Jossey-Bass Teacher

Jossey-Bass Teacher provides educators with practical knowledge and tools to create a positive and lifelong impact on student learning. We offer classroom-tested and research-based teaching resources for a variety of grade levels and subject areas. Whether you are an aspiring, new, or veteran teacher, we want to help you make every teaching day your best.

From ready-to-use classroom activities to the latest teaching framework, our value-packed books provide insightful, practical, and comprehensive materials on the topics that matter most to K–12 teachers. We hope to become your trusted source for the best ideas from the most experienced and respected experts in the field.

For more information about our resources, authors, and events please visit us at: www.josseybasseducation.com.

You may also find us on Facebook, Twitter, and Pinterest.

 Jossey-Bass K–12 Education

 jbeducation

Pinterest jbeducation

JB JOSSEY-BASS™
A Wiley Brand

The Elementary Teacher's Big Book of Graphic Organizers

100+ Ready-to-Use Organizers that Help Kids Learn Language Arts, Science, Social Studies, and More!

KATHERINE S. McKNIGHT

WILEY

Cover design: Michael Cook

Published by Jossey-Bass
A Wiley Imprint
One Montgomery Street, Suite 1200, San Francisco, CA 94104-4594—www.josseybass.com

Jossey-Bass books and products are available through most bookstores. To contact Jossey-Bass directly call our Customer Care Department within the U.S. at 800-956-7739, outside the U.S. at 317-572-3986, or fax 317-572-4002.

Wiley publishes in a variety of print and electronic formats and by print-on-demand. Some material included with standard print versions of this book may not be included in e-books or in print-on-demand. If this book refers to media such as a CD or DVD that is not included in the version you purchased, you may download this material at http://booksupport.wiley.com. For more information about Wiley products, visit www.wiley.com.

Library of Congress Cataloging-in-Publication Data has been applied for and is on file with the Library of Congress.

ISBN 978-1-118-34304-3 (paper), ISBN 978-1-118-41666-2 (ebk),
ISBN 978-1-118-42018-8 (ebk)

Printed in the United States of America

FIRST EDITION

PB Printing   10 9 8 7 6 5 4 3 2 1

CONTENTS

Chapter Four   Graphic Organizers for Note Taking and Study Skills   83

Chapter Five   Graphic Organizers for Literacy   117

Chapter Six   Graphic Organizers for Specific Subjects: Social Studies, Science, and Mathematics   187

For Jim, Ellie, and Colin, who bring joy to my life.

ACKNOWLEDGMENTS

My mom, a teacher for over thirty-five years in the Chicago Public Schools, would often remind me that teaching is an act of love and social justice. Her wise words are reminders to me of why we became teachers. It's always about our students and discovering the most effective teaching and learning strategies that will support our students to learn new skills and develop greater understandings. This volume is a resource that I hope will inspire and support effective and engaging teaching for the K–5 classroom.

There are many individuals whom I wish to thank who have supported my efforts to make this book a valuable teaching resource. Ellie McKnight, Celia Woldt, Laura Woldt, Olivia Doe, and Sydney Lawson were instrumental in making the student samples feature a success. I also need to thank Anna Johnson, who helped me discover the graphic possibilities of my ideas. Anna can make sense of my most muddled drawings and ideas and turn them into beautiful artistic representations. Elaine Carlson, a dear friend and fellow Girl Scout mom, offered her expert editing skills as I prepared the final manuscript. I also would like to thank my husband, Jim, whose love for me and patience for my work allows me to be the educator I want and need to be. Colin, my son, is a constant reminder that even when our work is challenging, we educators must remember that all children are beautifully different. I am also grateful for my daughter, Ellie, whose love of learning is infectious and inspiring. Ellie is always a good sport when I want to try our graphic organizer ideas with her and her friends.

I am grateful to the supportive staff at Jossey-Bass. Justin Frahm is masterful in the layout and production elements. It is a joy to work with an editor like Margie McAneny. This is the sixth book that she has edited with me, and no author could ask for a better editor than Margie.

Finally, I want to share my story of my sister's inspiration to so many writers. Mary Siewert Scruggs (1964–2011) was my sister, coauthor for *The Second City Guide to Improv in the Classroom*, and a great writer, performer, mom, wife, and teacher. She inspired a generation of writers through her work at Second City in Chicago and left a full legacy for one who left us too early. Mary was always the first person I turned to when I had to work out writing demons and challenges, and the first person I called when a new book was published. Because she was a great teacher, her words live on through the writing of so many others.

A MESSAGE FROM THE AUTHOR

Ever since I published my book *The Teacher's Big Book of Graphic Organizers, Grades 5–12* (recipient of the 2013 Teachers' Choice Award), I've had elementary teachers coming to me asking for a book they could use with their students. I drew upon my years of classroom experience, interviewed scores of elementary teachers and observed their classrooms, and even experimented on my own children and their friends. The result is this compendium of graphic organizers for students in grades K–5.

There are many tips and suggestions for using these graphic organizers throughout the book. But the strongest advice I can offer teachers and parents is to use your imaginations! There is rarely one and only one appropriate use for any organizer. I have organized them in a way that focuses on the skill set being developed, rather than just on the subject matter for which they are most appropriate. But the possible applications are many and varied. For example, the Food Chain Organizer (GO 41) can be useful for illustrating a sequence of events in science class, plotting a story in literacy class, identifying the steps in a math problem, or clarifying the important steps of a historical event. The vocabulary development organizers in Chapter Three can be used as tools for mastering new vocabulary in any subject. A Venn diagram (GO 2 and GO 3) is useful whether comparing two fictional characters in literature class or two cloud formations in science class. All of the cause-and-effect graphic organizers (GO 4, GO 5, and GO 90) are valuable, whether a student is considering the details of an American Revolutionary War battle, the effect of rain on a desert, or a fictionalized account of St. George slaying a dragon. In the final chapter I include a number of graphic organizers that have been developed with specific content matter in mind. But even these—social studies graphic organizers, science graphic organizers, and mathematics graphic organizers—can sometimes have applications in other areas of study. Elementary school students are creative and malleable, and these graphic organizers can match them turn for turn.

Katie

Dr. Katherine McKnight

ABOUT THE AUTHOR

Katherine S. McKnight, Ph.D., began her career as a high school English teacher in the Chicago Public School system. She currently serves as a professor of secondary education at National Louis University and an onsite professional development consultant for the National Council of Teachers of English (NCTE). Katie is passionate about creating curricula that engage all students in the regular education classroom. She is committed to the development, sharing, and promotion of ideas and strategies that develop literacy skills in adolescent students so that they can grow to be active, creative adults.

Katie publishes regularly in professional journals and is the author of numerous books including *The Teacher's Big Book of Graphic Organizers, Grades 5–12* (recipient of the 2013 Teachers' Choice Award from *Learning* Magazine); *The English Teacher's Survival Guide, 2nd Edition* (with Mary Lou Brandvik); *The Second City Guide to Improve in the Classroom* (with Mary Scruggs); and *Teaching English in Middle and Secondary Schools, 5th Edition* (with Rhoda Maxwell and Mary Meiser).

To learn more, go to www.katherinemcknight.com.

CHAPTER ONE

What Are Graphic Organizers and Why Are They So Important for Teaching and Learning?

Graphic organizers are visual representations of information and concepts. By nature, we tend to learn in pictures; as such, the graphic organizer is a more innate structure for processing information than recording information exclusively in words. In addition, because graphic organizers use visual images and words, they are more effective tools for learning for a wide variety of learners, such as English language learners and students with special needs.

Why are graphic organizers such effective teaching and learning tools?

- They help students to focus on important and key information.
- We learn in pictures, and graphic organizers are a visual representation of newly learned material.
- Graphic organizers help us organize content information.
- Businesses and professional organizations often use graphic organizers to represent content. As students become able to create, interpret, analyze, and synthesize information graphically, they are developing important skills in visual literacy.
- We can use graphic organizers for assessment. Students can represent what they know and understand in a graphic organizer. I always advise teachers to instruct their students to write an explanation, description, or narrative of the graphic organizer, explaining why certain information is included and how it's organized.

• When students are exposed to a wide variety of graphic organizers, they become more willing to use them for note taking and studying.

How Is This Book Organized?

Each graphic organizer is presented with an overview, tips for classroom implementation, and student samples.

Overview

In the overview of each strategy for each organizer, you will see a graphic that illustrates the complexity or challenge of each: easy, medium, or hard. The overview also contains instructional information to increase the effectiveness of each graphic organizer in the classroom.

Tips for Classroom Implementation

This section of each organizer presents specific information and suggestions for implementing the graphic organizer in classroom practice. The following general classroom implementation tips apply to all graphic organizers:

• "I Do, We Do, You Do" is an instructional strategy wherein the teacher models the completion of the graphic organizer in the "I Do" step; in "We Do," the students use the graphic organizer with the teacher's guidance and modeling; and in the "You Do" stage, the students are ready to use the graphic organizer independently.

• Consider making three-dimensional models of the graphic organizers using construction paper and markers. You'll find examples of these three-dimensional graphic organizers throughout the book. This kind of organizer is especially appealing for visual and kinesthetic learners.

• Model the use of different colored markers and pencils for the information and content recorded on the graphic organizer, and encourage your students to use them. Color-coding is a useful strategy for all kinds of learners; it is particularly beneficial for students with special needs, who may have a disability that makes informational organization more challenging.

• Experiment with and use a wide variety of graphic organizers. There are many ways to organize information. Demonstrate and motivate your students to try multiple graphic organizers and strategies so that they can think critically about information in a wide variety of ways.

• If you are using graphic organizers with your students for the first time (as in the beginning of the school year), I suggest that you begin with more simple graphic organizers. Once the students master these, begin to implement increasingly more difficult and complex ones. Also, encourage your students to create their own graphic organizers or make adaptations to the ones that you provide.

• When students are working in groups and using graphic organizers, remind them of the skills that are important for effective collaborative learning. For example, model and discuss turn-taking, questioning, listening, speaking, and respecting each member of the group.

• Encourage discussion of the concepts and relationships that are represented in the graphic organizers. These associations are important for student learning.

• Model and remind students that the same information can be represented in many different ways.

• Include vocabulary, pictures, and icons in graphic organizers to place greater emphasis on key information and relationships to help English language learners and students with special needs grasp concepts.

- When using graphic organizers for assessment, make sure that students have already used them in your classroom. Asking students to create graphic organizers to represent what they know, understand, and comprehend is also effective. Students who have special needs and may have a disability that makes writing difficult can more easily complete a graphic organizer, which requires less writing, to demonstrate their understanding of content. You might also consider conducting a mini conference with the students so they have the opportunity to explain the relationships and associations of the material.
- Create an information sheet to send home to parents explaining the structure and purpose of graphic organizers being used during instruction. When parents understand the purpose of graphic organizers, they can support their child's learning. Encourage parents to use the graphic organizers at home with their children.

Student Samples

The book provides student samples to demonstrate some possible responses to each graphic organizer. These samples were created by K–5 students.

Summary

Graphic organizers are an effective teaching and learning tool for all types of learners. These organizational frameworks support students' thinking and comprehension and also stimulate social interactions.

I believe in the power of graphic organizers, which is supported by many researchers. When graphic organizers become part of instruction, there is a greater emphasis on more inquiry, process, and critical-thinking learning. Better questioning, reasoning, and thinking become more evident among students and teachers. Teachers often report that when they begin to use graphic organizers in class, students have a better understanding and retention of newly learned content.

Using a wide variety of teaching and learning strategies leads to the most successful and engaging classroom experiences for students. Graphic organizers are one type of strategy. I hope that the over one hundred strategies in this book will support you in meeting the needs of the varied learners within your classroom.

You can download PDF versions of many of the graphic organizers found in this book at
www.josseybass.com/go/elementaryGO
Password: 56jm29

CHAPTER TWO
Graphic Organizers for Brainstorming and Idea Generation

1 ABC Brainstorm

▶ Grades: 2–5
▶ Level of Difficulty: Medium

Overview

The ABC Brainstorm graphic organizer prompts students to recall and brainstorm information. Use of the ABC format facilitates the organization of information. Students are prompted to record information for each letter, requiring them to dig deeply into prior knowledge about the concept in order to complete this exercise.

Tips for Classroom Implementation

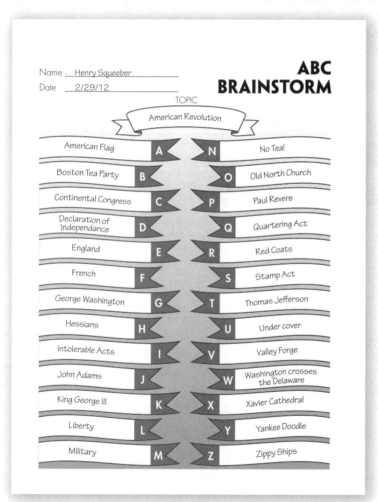

ABC Brainstorm is a highly versatile graphic organizer that can be applied to before, during, and after reading instructional situations. As an introductory prereading activity, the ABC Brainstorm facilitates the recall of previous information as students explore new content. While a text is being read, key information can be recorded with each corresponding letter. As an after reading or as a culminating unit activity, the ABC Brainstorm graphic organizer supports students to review and assess what they recall and learned.

The students may have some difficulty finding information that begins with the letters Q and X. Students can include adjectives and use Q or X as a letter within a word or phrase (see sample).

The students may also enjoy creating an alphabet picture book, using the information from the ABC Brainstorm. Each page would represent the letter, corresponding information, and visuals.

ABC BRAINSTORM

Name _____

Date _____

TOPIC

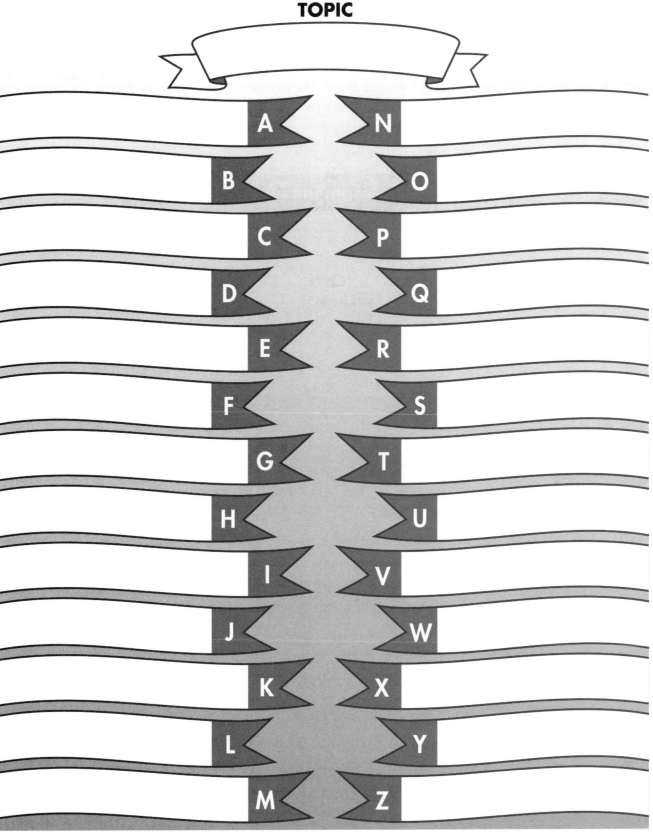

2 Venn Diagram 1

▶ Grades: K–5
▶ Level of Difficulty: Easy

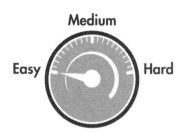

Overview

The Venn diagram is one of the most well-known graphic organizers. This useful and adaptable graphic organizer provides a visual comparison of similarities and differences between subjects. The structure of this organizer is applicable to a wide variety of topics.

Tips for Classroom Implementation

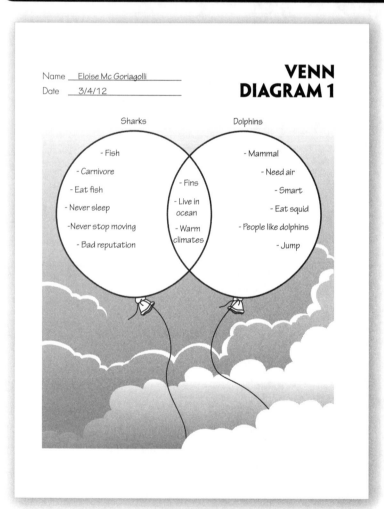

Name Eloise Mc Goriagolli
Date 3/4/12

VENN DIAGRAM 1

Sharks
- Fish
- Carnivore
- Eat fish
- Never sleep
- Never stop moving
- Bad reputation

- Fins
- Live in ocean
- Warm climates

Dolphins
- Mammal
- Need air
- Smart
- Eat squid
- People like dolphins
- Jump

A Venn diagram can be easily adapted to include more than two topics and one common area. Once the students complete the Venn diagram, they should discuss what they included in the circles and the common area. These discussions can be completed in large and small group discussions.

The middle area where the two circles overlap can be tricky. Sometimes the students become confused and continue to put opposites or comparisons in this place. Using different colored markers or pencils for each circle and the overlapping intersection is a simple adaptation that allows students to see the differences and similarities in the presented information from the onset.

Another adaptation is to instruct the students to cut out two circles. The students can write the characteristics for each area and then glue the circles to create a Venn diagram.

Name _____

Date _____

3 Venn Diagram 2

▶ Grades: 2–5
▶ Level of Difficulty: Medium-Hard

Overview

See the overview for Graphic Organizer 2, Venn Diagram 1. This Venn diagram is a more advanced model that students can use to make more advanced comparisons between three sources of information.

Tips for Classroom Implementation

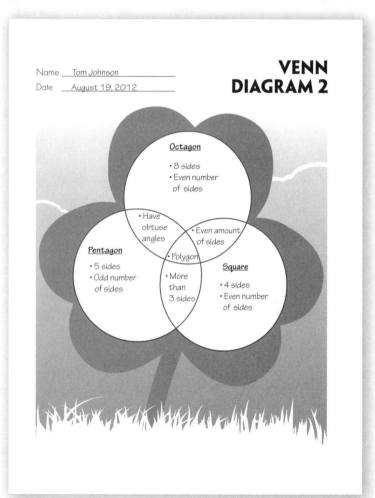

Once students have mastered the Venn Diagram 1, introduce this more complex version. I also suggest that you could use both Venn Diagram 1 and 2 in a center. You can differentiate instruction by providing students with two versions to meet the needs of different levels of learners.

As mentioned for Venn Diagram 1, have the students cut out the different circles to create a multidimensional representation.

Name _____

Date _____

VENN DIAGRAM 2

4 Cause and Effect 1

► Grades: K–5
► Level of Difficulty: Medium

Overview

The Cause and Effect graphic organizer facilitates categorizations and connections among a large body of information. This kind of organizer is especially useful for subjects such as science and social studies. Students' ability to identify causes and effects promotes higher-level thinking (synthesizing and analyzing information).

Tips for Classroom Implementation

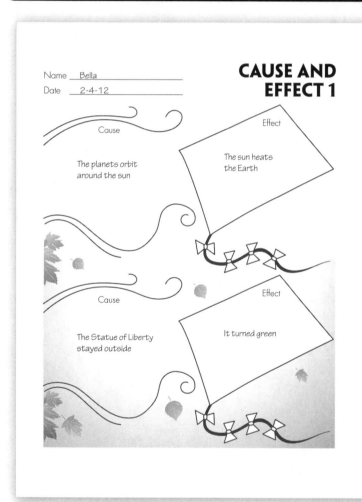

Students will record corresponding information regarding causes and effects for a unit of study or body of information. I like to use different colored markers and pens to help the students distinguish between the causes and effects in this graphic organizer. Color coding is especially useful for students with special needs where a disability may make it challenging to categorize and track information.

Here are some additional suggestions for using this graphic organizer:

- Have the students work in pairs.
- Project the graphic organizer on an interactive whiteboard and use it in a center as a formative assessment of students' understanding of newly presented content.
- Use the graphic organizer as an end-of-the-unit assessment.

You can also create a three-dimensional form of this graphic organizer.

CAUSE AND EFFECT 1

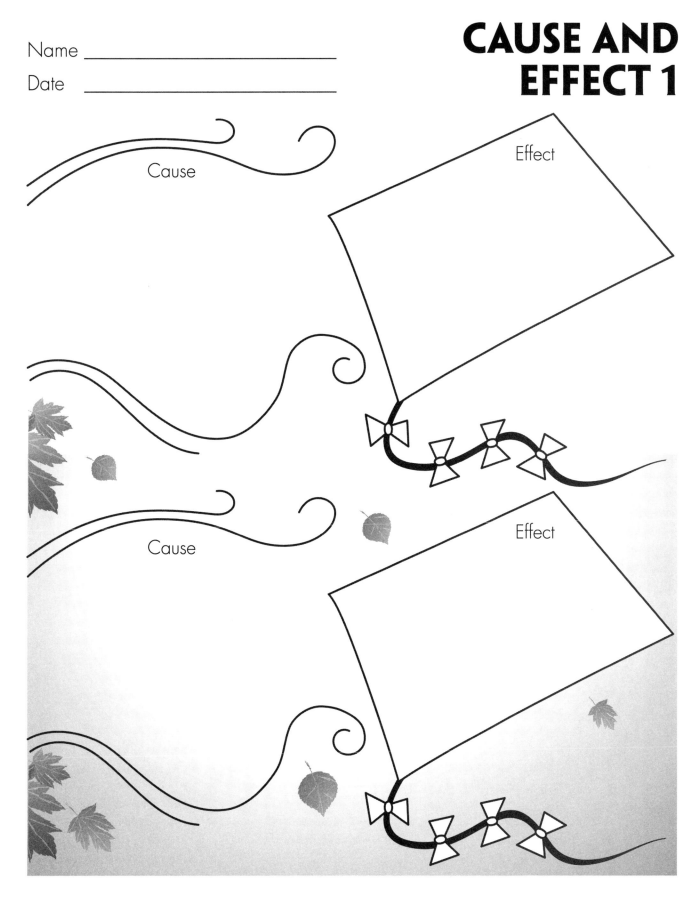

Cause

Effect

Cause

Effect

5 Cause and Effect 2

▶ Grades: K–5
▶ Level of Difficulty: Hard

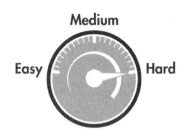

Overview

See the overview for Graphic Organizer 4, Cause and Effect 1.

Tips for Classroom Implementation

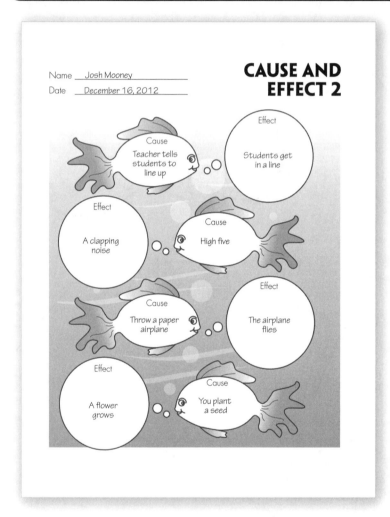

You can use both Cause and Effect 1 and Cause and Effect 2 graphic organizers as a means to differentiate instruction among differently abled learners. I have used both organizers in a learning center; the students choose, or I might assign either Cause and Effect 1 or Cause and Effect 2 for the students to complete.

Name _____

Date _____

CAUSE AND EFFECT 2

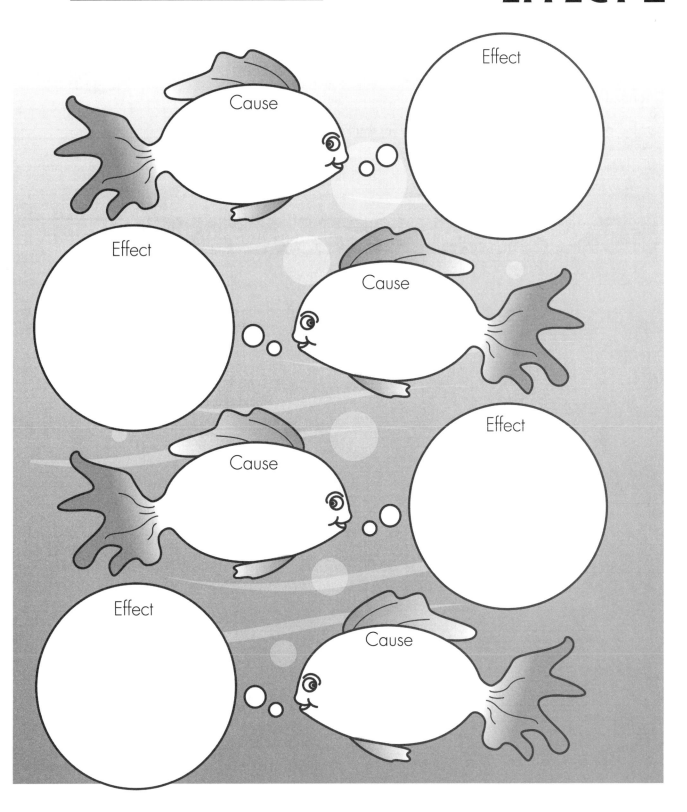

6 Compare and Contrast 1

▶ Grades: K–5
▶ Level of Difficulty: Medium

Overview

Comparing and contrasting information is often challenging for students because it requires them to go beyond simply recalling and listing information. As students compare and contrast information, they have to analyze the information and consider the ways in which it is similar and different. These are much higher-level thinking skills than the simple recalling of information.

Tips for Classroom Implementation

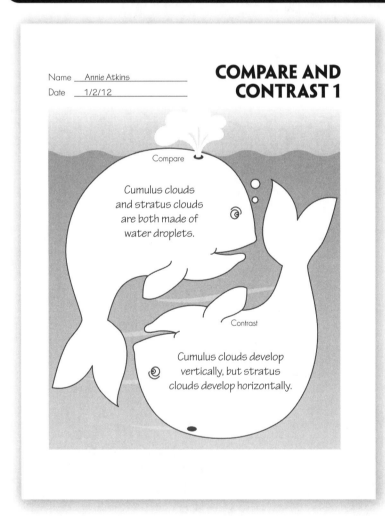

As with the Cause and Effect 1 and 2 graphic organizers, I like to instruct the students to use different colored markers or pens for the causes and effects. It helps the students to categorize the information and offers students a visualized cueing of the similarities and differences for the body of information that they are analyzing.

Students also enjoy creating three-dimensional representations of this kind of graphic organizer.

Compare

Contrast

7   Compare and Contrast 2

▶ Grades: K–5
▶ Level of Difficulty: Hard

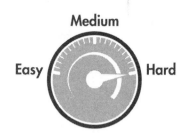

Overview

See the overview for Graphic Organizer 6, Compare and Contrast 1.

Tips for Classroom Implementation

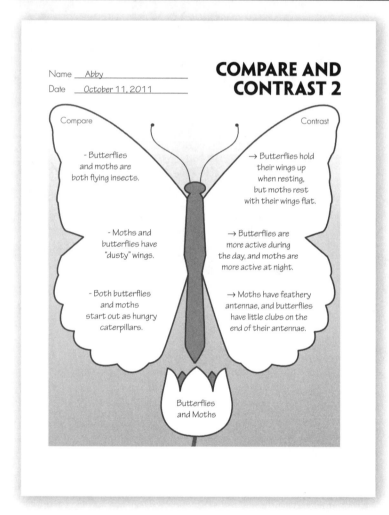

This is a more challenging graphic organizer than Compare and Contrast 1. I like to use this graphic organizer with Compare and Contrast 1 as a means to differentiate and provide a challenge to students. You can use both of these Compare and Contrast graphic organizers at a learning center.

Remember that you can also create three-dimensional models with construction papers and use different colored markers and pens for the compare and contrast exercise.

Name _____

Date _____

COMPARE AND CONTRAST 2

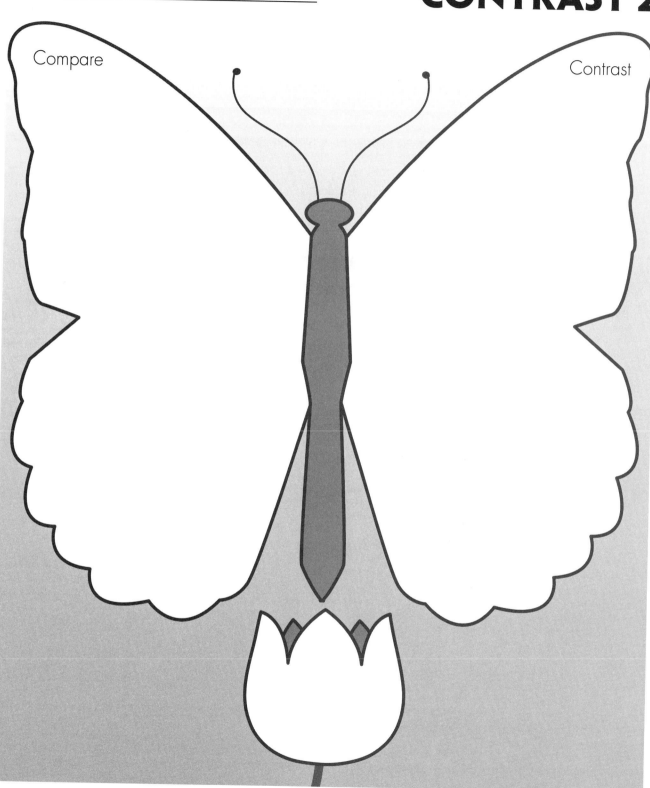

Compare

Contrast

8 KWL 1

► Grades: K–5
► Level of Difficulty: Easy

Overview

Created by Donna Ogle, the KWL strategy is a three-column chart that captures the before, during, and after stages of reading. This three-column chart can also be used as a preview for a new unit.

K = What a reader or student *knows* about the selected topic. Students tap prior knowledge before reading. As we know from research in reading, prior knowledge supports student comprehension.

W = What a student *wants* to know about the selected topic. Asking questions before reading or beginning a unit of study boosts comprehension.

L = What the students *learned* about the topic. Students are better able to synthesize newly acquired information when given an opportunity to reflect and make connections between their prior knowledge and information recently attained.

Tips for Classroom Implementation

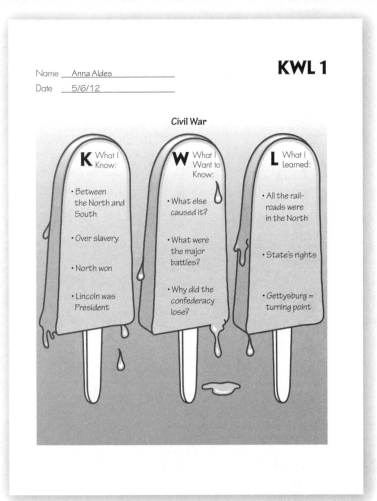

The KWL strategy is one of the most widely recognized graphic organizers and instructional strategies. It is best used at the beginning of a unit of study or reading. Highly adaptable, it can be used for individual, small, or large group instruction. Remember, when students tap into prior knowledge and pose individual questions, they are more likely to become engaged in their learning and more apt to internalize what they are studying and learning.

To support all kinds of learners, consider using different colored markers or pens for the three different columns. You could also have the students create the three columns from different colored paper and paste each column on a larger sheet of paper. This would be especially engaging for visual and kinesthetic learners.

Name _____

Date _____

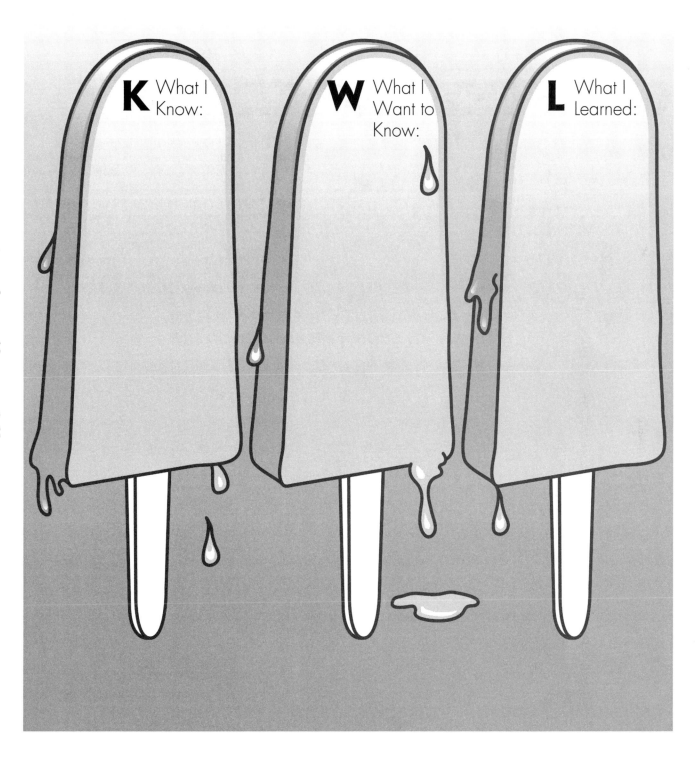

K What I Know:

W What I Want to Know:

L What I Learned:

9 KWL 2

► Grades: K–5
► Level of Difficulty: Easy

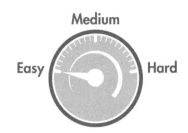

Overview

See the overview for Graphic Organizer 8, KWL 1.

Tips for Classroom Implementation

Name _Ginger Price_

Date _October 3, 2012_

KWL 2

K What I Know: The book is called _Charlotte's Web_, and the pig and a spider are characters

W What I Want to Know: How Wilbur meets the spider and how he is saved

L What I Learned: That Wilbur is saved by Charlotte the spider

This is a more challenging graphic organizer than KWL 1. I like to use this graphic organizer with KWL 1 as a means to differentiate and provide options for students. You can use both of these KWL graphic organizers at a learning center.

Remember that you can also create three-dimensional models with construction papers and use different colored markers and pens for the different columns.

Name _____

Date _____

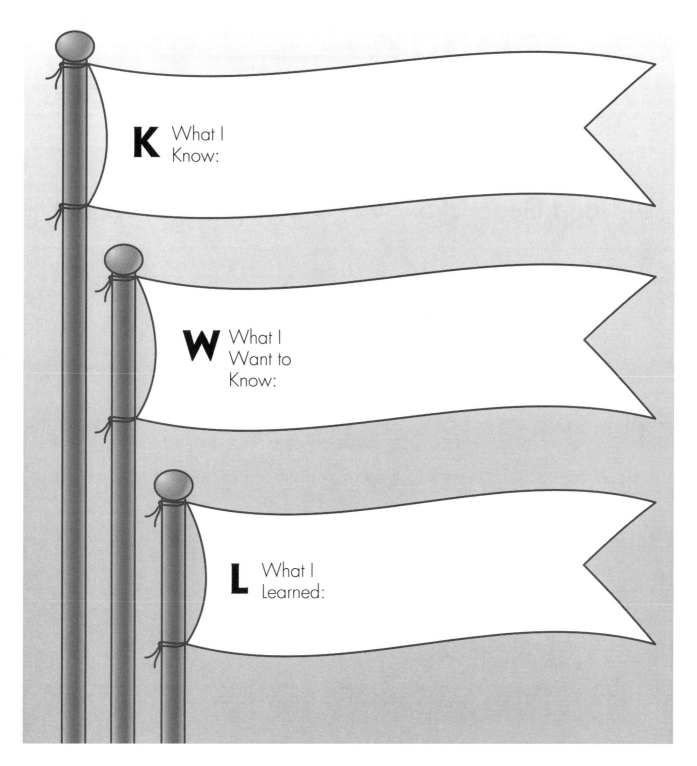

K What I
Know:

W What I
Want to
Know:

L What I
Learned:

Graphic Organizers 10–17: Idea Generation

Overview

Graphic Organizers 10–17 visualize and organize ideas and prior knowledge. These graphic organizers have a wide variety of applications, especially for writing, questioning, and thinking about new information.

Tips for Classroom Implementation

When students tap into prior knowledge and brainstorm, they are more likely to become engaged in what they are learning and studying. Remember it is always helpful to model this kind of graphic organizer through a Think Aloud. In a Think Aloud, teachers model their own thinking and complete the graphic organizer for the students on an overhead projector, LCD projector, or similar means of projection.

For students who may have challenges with focus and concentration, it's also helpful to display only one section of the graphic organizer at a time. This facilitates the student's ability to focus and concentrate.

10   Idea Generation with 4 Ideas: Linear Model

▶ Grades: K–5
▶ Level of Difficulty: Easy

IDEA GENERATION WITH 4 IDEAS:
LINEAR MODEL

11 Idea Generation with 6 Ideas: Linear Model

▶ Grades: 2–5
▶ Level of Difficulty: Medium

Overview

See the notes at the beginning of this section.

Tips for Classroom Implementation

See the notes at the beginning of this section.

Name _____

Date _____

IDEA GENERATION WITH 6 IDEAS: LINEAR MODEL

12   Idea Generation with 3 Ideas: Circle Model

▶ Grades: K–5
▶ Level of Difficulty: Easy

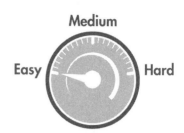

Overview

See the notes at the beginning of this section.

Tips for Classroom Implementation

See the notes at the beginning of this section.

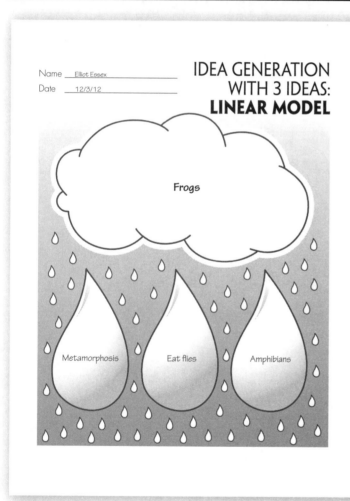

Name ___Elliot Essex___

Date ___12/3/12___

IDEA GENERATION
WITH 3 IDEAS:
LINEAR MODEL

Frogs

Metamorphosis   Eat flies   Amphibians

Name _____

Date _____

IDEA GENERATION WITH 3 IDEAS: LINEAR MODEL

13   Idea Generation with 4 Ideas: Circle Model

▶ Grades: 2–5
▶ Level of Difficulty: Medium

Overview

See the notes at the beginning of this section.

Tips for Classroom Implementation

See the notes at the beginning of this section.

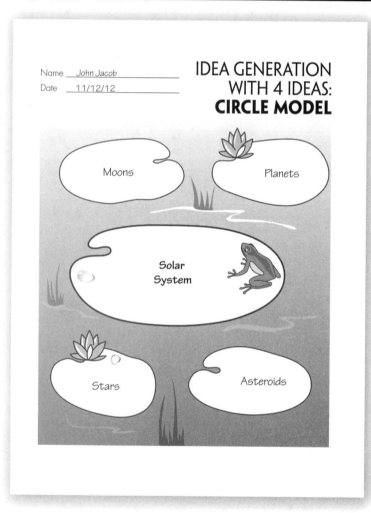

Name _____

Date _____

14 Idea Generation with 6 Ideas: Circle Model

▶ Grades: 2–5
▶ Level of Difficulty: Hard

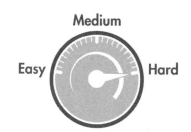

Overview

See the notes at the beginning of this section.

 Tips for Classroom Implementation

See the notes at the beginning of this section.

Name _____

Date _____

15 Idea Generation: Tree Design

▶ Grades: K–5
▶ Level of Difficulty: Medium

Overview

See the notes at the beginning of this section.

Tips for Classroom Implementation

See the notes at the beginning of this section.

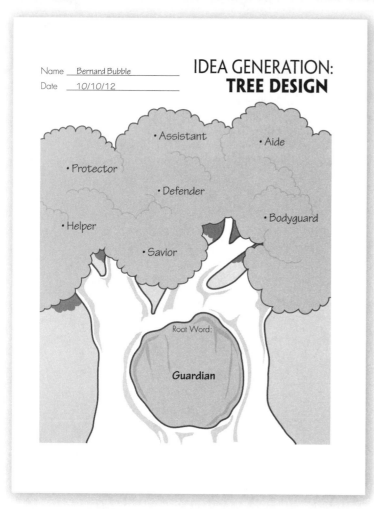

Name _____

Date _____

IDEA GENERATION:
TREE DESIGN

Root Word:

16 Idea Generation: Flower Petal Design

▶ Grades: K–5
▶ Level of Difficulty: Medium

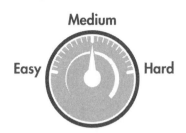

Overview

See the notes at the beginning of this section.

Tips for Classroom Implementation

See the notes at the beginning of this section.

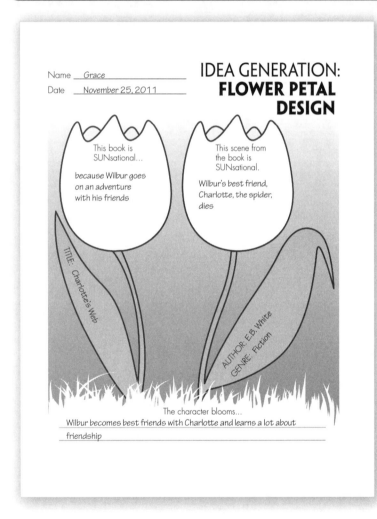

Name _____

Date _____

IDEA GENERATION:
FLOWER PETAL DESIGN

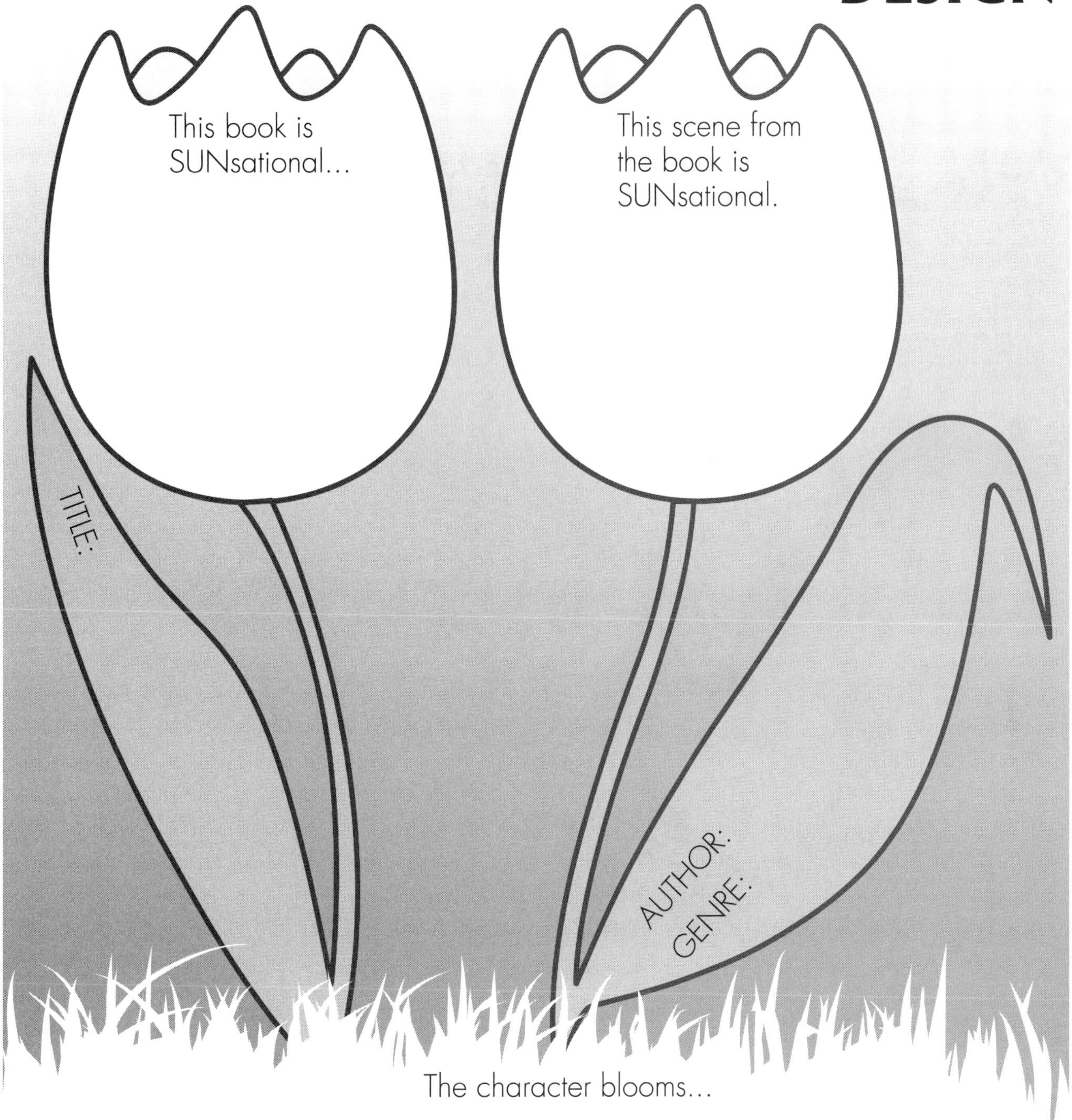

This book is SUNsational…

This scene from the book is SUNsational.

TITLE:

AUTHOR:

GENRE:

The character blooms…

_____

_____

17 Idea Generation: Hand Model

▶ Grades: 2–5
▶ Level of Difficulty: Medium

Overview

See the notes at the beginning of this section.

Tips for Classroom Implementation

See the notes at the beginning of this section.

Name _____

Date _____

IDEA GENERATION:
HAND MODEL

18 Anticipation Guide

► Grades: 2–5
► Level of Difficulty: Easy

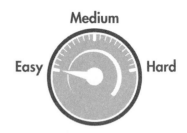

Overview

An anticipation guide is a previewing organizer that prompts students to draw from previous knowledge prior to the study and exploration of new material.

For prereaders, you can use pictures that students can examine and circle either a happy or sad face to indicate either feelings about the picture or figure (see the anticipation guide on page 41).

For readers, see the anticipation guide on page 43. Provide teacher-created statements that prompt students to draw from prior knowledge and conclude whether they "agree" or "disagree" with the statements.

For either anticipation guide, use the students' responses at the end of the unit of study or reading. Ask the students to reconsider their previous responses. Discuss the students' verifications or rejections of previous responses as a metacognitive exercise.

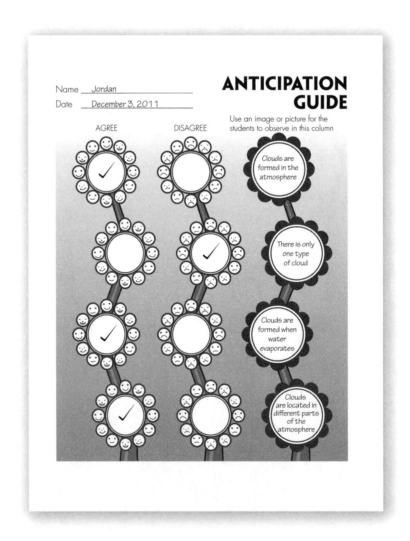

Name _____

Date _____

ANTICIPATION GUIDE

Use an image or picture for the
students to observe in this column

AGREE   DISAGREE

Copyright © 2013 by John Wiley & Sons, Inc.

Name   Denny McDonald

Date   9/30/12

ANTICIPATION GUIDE

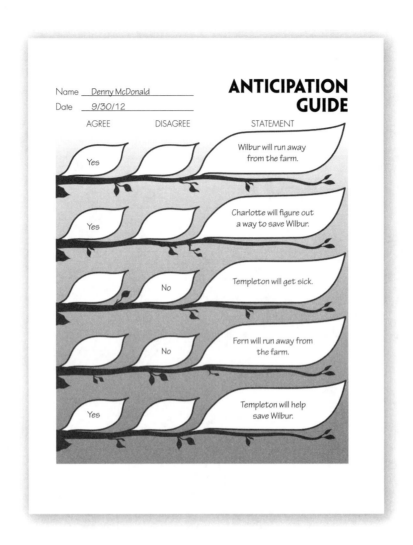

AGREE   DISAGREE   STATEMENT

Yes   Wilbur will run away
                            from the farm.

Yes   Charlotte will figure out
                            a way to save Wilbur.

          No   Templeton will get sick.

          No   Fern will run away from
                            the farm.

Yes   Templeton will help
                            save Wilbur.

ANTICIPATION GUIDE

Name _____

Date _____

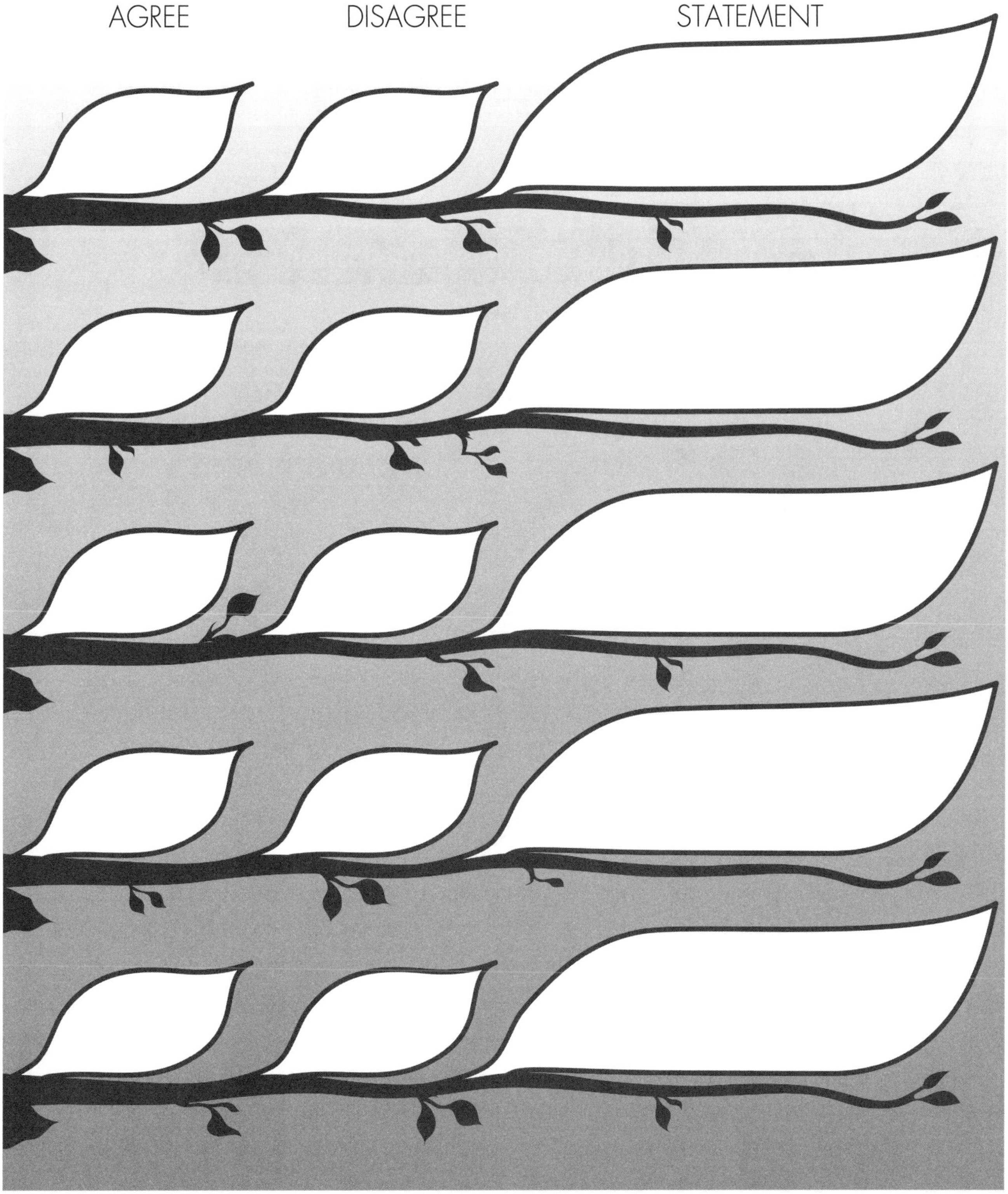

AGREE   DISAGREE   STATEMENT

19 Previewer

▶ Grades: 2–5
▶ Level of Difficulty: Easy

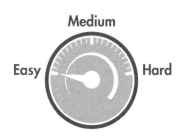

Overview

When students activate and draw from prior knowledge, they are able to create and pose engaging questions that help them to be more thoughtful and engaged readers and thinkers.

Tips for Classroom Implementation

Name   Gordon

Date   November 15, 2012

PREVIEWER

What I already know about the topic is…

Thomas Edison created and tested the light bulb. He couldn't find the correct filament. He tested over 100 filaments.

TOPIC: Thomas Edison

Prior to reading or learning new material, ask students to record what they may already know about the topic. Instruct the students that while they read and study the topic, they can pose new questions, answer their previously posed questions, and confirm or reject original ideas and assumptions.

As the students preview content, prompt them to examine images, pictures, and words.

PREVIEWER

Name _____

Date _____

What I already know
about the topic is…

TOPIC:

20 Summarizer/Main Idea

▶ Grades: K–5
▶ Level of Difficulty: Medium-Hard

Overview

Identifying supporting details in informational texts and then synthesizing into a summative statement or main idea is the highest level of understanding.

Tips for Classroom Implementation

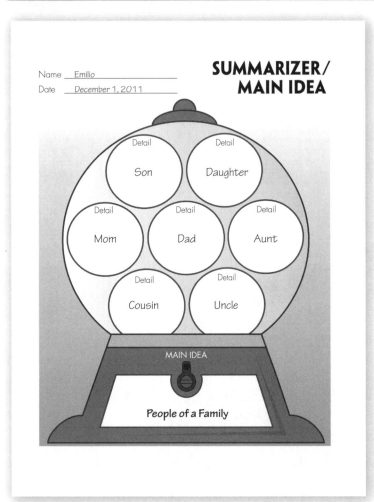

Name __Emilio__
Date __December 1, 2011__

SUMMARIZER/ MAIN IDEA

Detail — Son
Detail — Daughter
Detail — Mom
Detail — Dad
Detail — Aunt
Detail — Cousin
Detail — Uncle

MAIN IDEA

People of a Family

As the students read an informational text, have them identify and record the supporting details on each of the gumballs in Graphic Organizer 20. Once the students have recorded the details, instruct them to discuss the information in pairs. Still in pairs, the students can then compose a statement that articulates the main idea.

SUMMARIZER/ MAIN IDEA

Detail

Detail

Detail

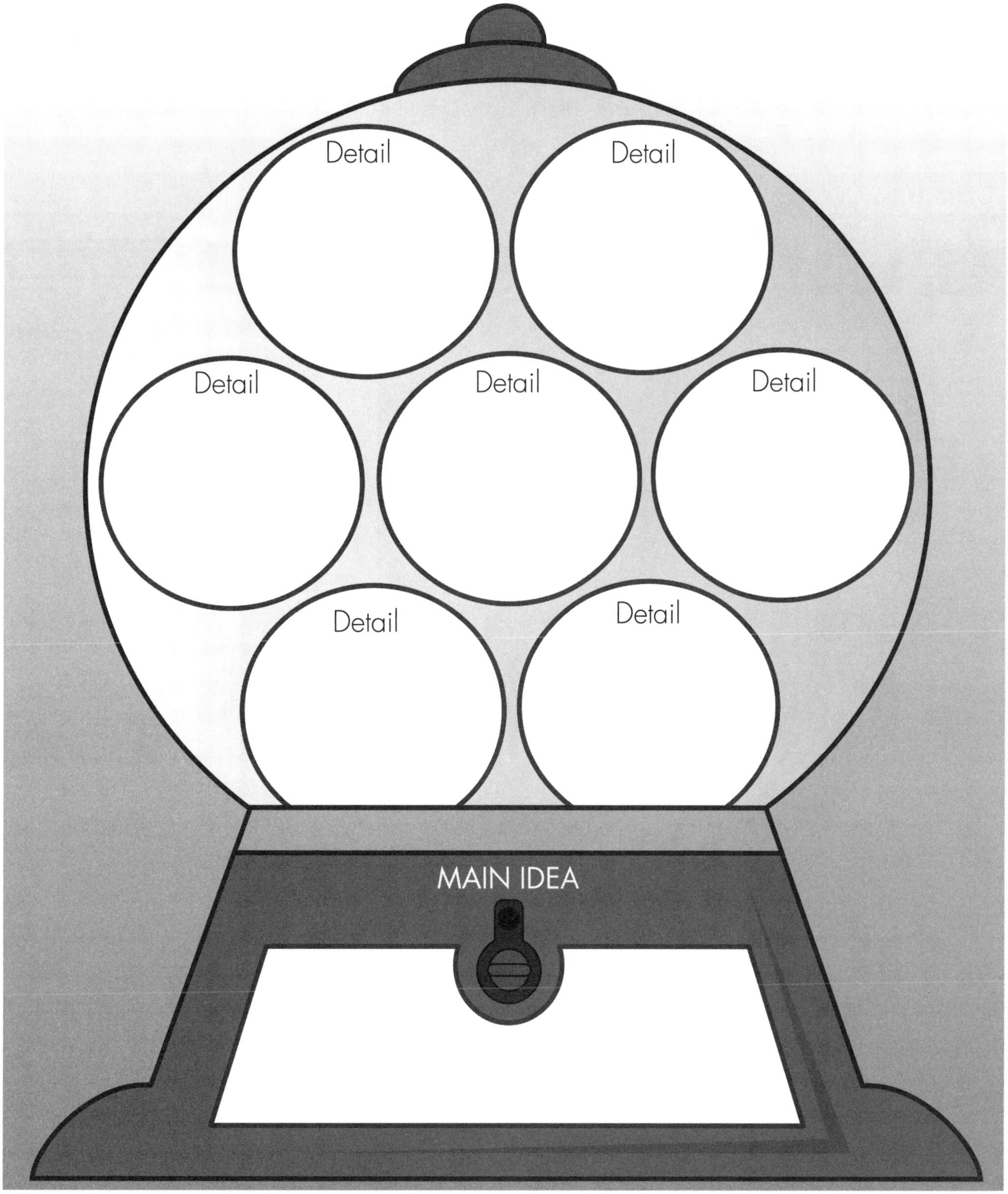

Detail

Detail

Detail

Detail

MAIN IDEA

21 Idea Web

▶ Grades: K–5
▶ Level of Difficulty: Medium

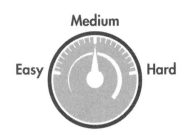

Overview

Also known as a mind map, the Idea Web records students' ideas and the associations and connections between these ideas. This graphic organizer is especially useful for visual learners.

Tips for Classroom Implementation

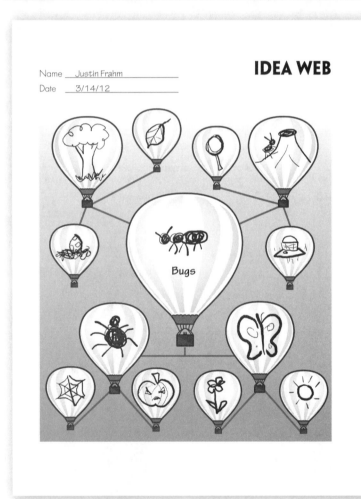

This activity can be conducted through large or small group instruction using the following directions:

- Select a topic.
- Create a drawing or image that represents the topic.
- The topic and corresponding drawing or image should be at the center of the web.
- Discuss and brainstorm examples, key concepts, and ideas associated with the main topic.
- Add lines to connect ideas and key words.
- Using different colored pencils and markers helps students to make associations. Graphic Organizer 21 provides a rough outline as a starting point for students. You can also use a large sheet of paper and have students add to it throughout a unit of study. This would document students' learning and be a foundation for unit review.

Name _____

Date _____

22 Fishbone

▶ Grades: 3–5
▶ Level of Difficulty: Medium-Hard

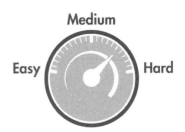

Overview

The Fishbone graphic organizer helps students to organize and connect details so that they can identify the main idea in informational text.

Tips for Classroom Implementation

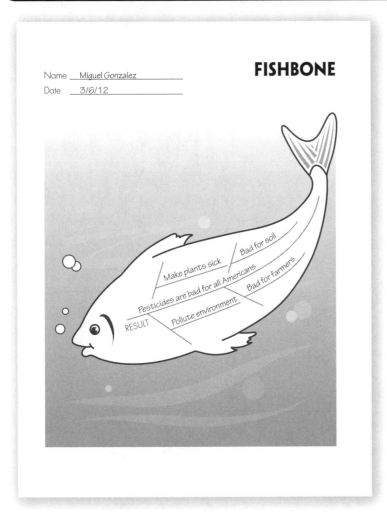

Name Miguel Gonzalez
Date 3/6/12

FISHBONE

Make plants sick
Bad for soil
Pesticides are bad for all Americans
Bad for farmers
RESULT
Pollute environment

Once the students have read the text, instruct them to identify the main idea on the spine of the Fishbone graphic organizer. The students should write corresponding details on the other bones.

This graphic organizer can also be used for prewriting. The students can begin with the main idea or thesis on the spine and then list details and evidence on the other bones.

Name _____

Date _____

RESULT

23 Herringbone

▶ Grades: 3–5
▶ Level of Difficulty: Medium-Hard

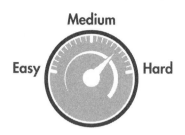

Overview

Like the Fishbone graphic organizer, the Herringbone graphic organizer helps students to understand the connections between supporting details to identify a main idea. The Herringbone is a useful graphic organizer for students to organize information.

Tips for Classroom Implementation

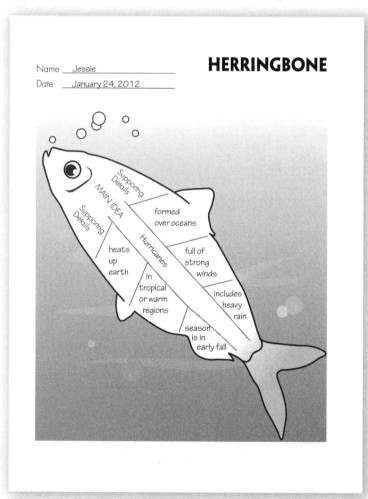

Learning how to organize and classify information so that they can summarize and identify main ideas is an important skill for students. They learn and develop this skill every day when they are asked to identify key information and prompted to synthesize it into a summative statement or main idea.

Using different colored markers and pens will help students to distinguish between the information. Also, it is always important to model for the students new graphic organizers and strategies for recording and organizing information. This graphic organizer will especially appeal to visual learners.

HERRINGBONE

Name _____

Date _____

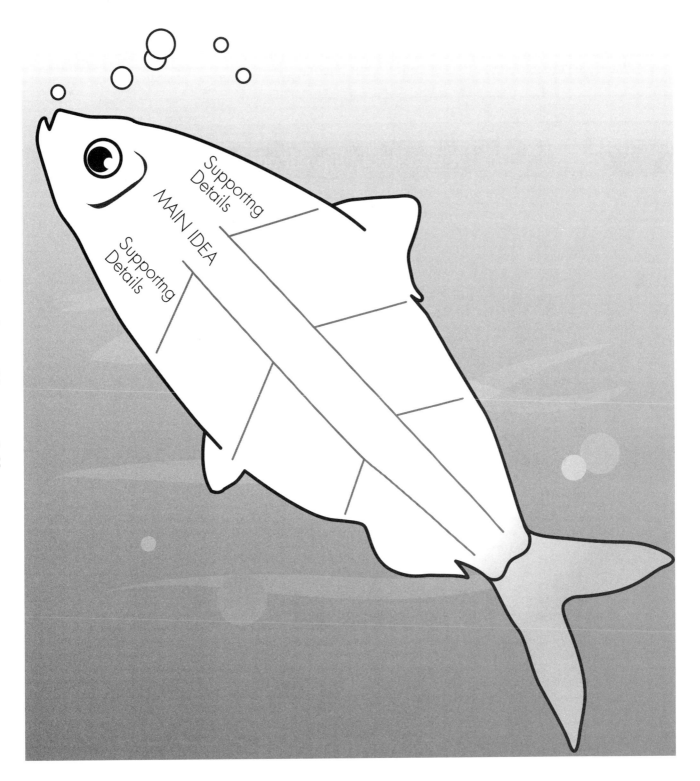

Supporting
Details

MAIN IDEA

Supporting
Details

24   Y Diagram

▶ Grades: 2–5
▶ Level of Difficulty: Medium

Overview

The Y graphic organizer supports students' visualization of how ideas or details can support a main idea. It is a more simplified supporting details/main idea organizer than the Fishbone or Herringbone.

Tips for Classroom Implementation

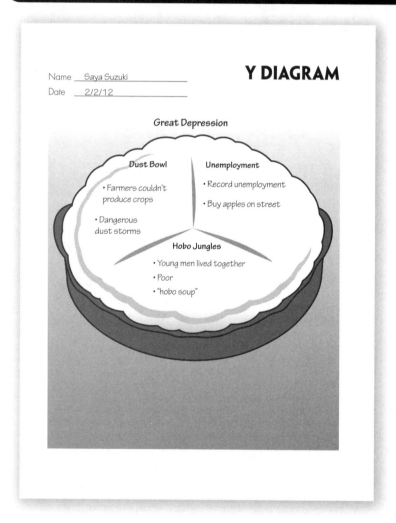

Name   Saya Suzuki
Date   2/2/12

Y DIAGRAM

Great Depression

Dust Bowl
• Farmers couldn't produce crops
• Dangerous dust storms

Unemployment
• Record unemployment
• Buy apples on street

Hobo Jungles
• Young men lived together
• Poor
• "hobo soup"

I like to use this organizer as a prewriting activity. Students can record what they already know about a topic. Students record details and information about the topic; then they can create a main focus or topic for their writing. I think it is also helpful for students to share their prewriting organization. It builds the community of student writers, and it is useful for peers to observe how we all can organize information differently.

Model this organizer for the students before they use it independently. Also, using different colored markers and pens for each line can support visual learners even further.

Y DIAGRAM

Name _____

Date _____

CHAPTER THREE

Graphic Organizers for Vocabulary Development

25 Vocabulary Slide 1

▶ Grades: K–5
▶ Level of Difficulty: Medium

Overview

I remember learning new vocabulary. My teachers would require that I write each word three to five times, record the definition, and write a sentence using the new word. After the quiz, usually given on a Friday, I forgot most of the words. That traditional method for teaching vocabulary is ineffective. Through extensive research in language learning, we know that learning new words and concepts must be contextualized in order to increase retention.

The more students play with words, the more likely they will internalize and use the new vocabulary. The Vocabulary Slide graphic organizer is designed to promote understanding of a concept or new word. Although more traditional methods may take less time in the classroom, those strategies are ineffective for learning vocabulary. The Vocabulary Slide is far more effective, as it promotes deep understanding and retention.

Tips for Classroom Implementation

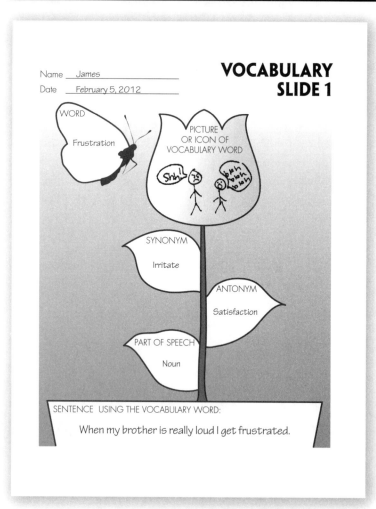

Using the butterfly graphic organizer, select a vocabulary word or concept and write it in the central part of the butterfly. The words can be selected by either the teachers or the students. Then fill in the flower, leaves, and dish with the corresponding picture, words, and sentence.

Name _____

Date _____

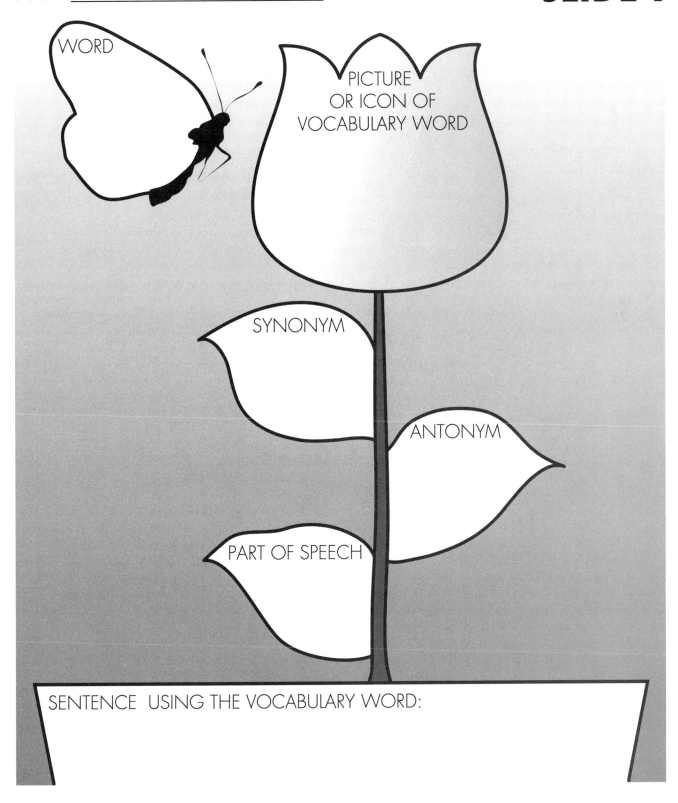

WORD

PICTURE
OR ICON OF
VOCABULARY WORD

SYNONYM

ANTONYM

PART OF SPEECH

SENTENCE USING THE VOCABULARY WORD:

26 Vocabulary Slide 2

▶ Grades: 2–5
▶ Level of Difficulty: Medium

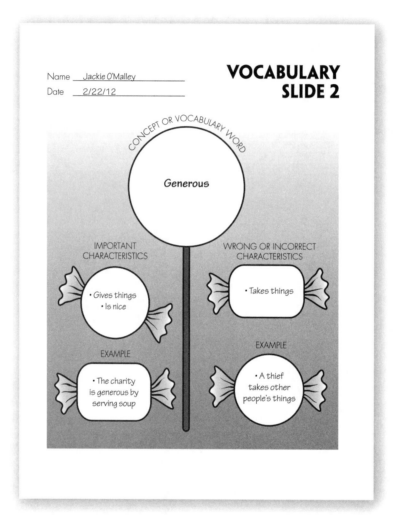

Name _____

Date _____

VOCABULARY
SLIDE 2

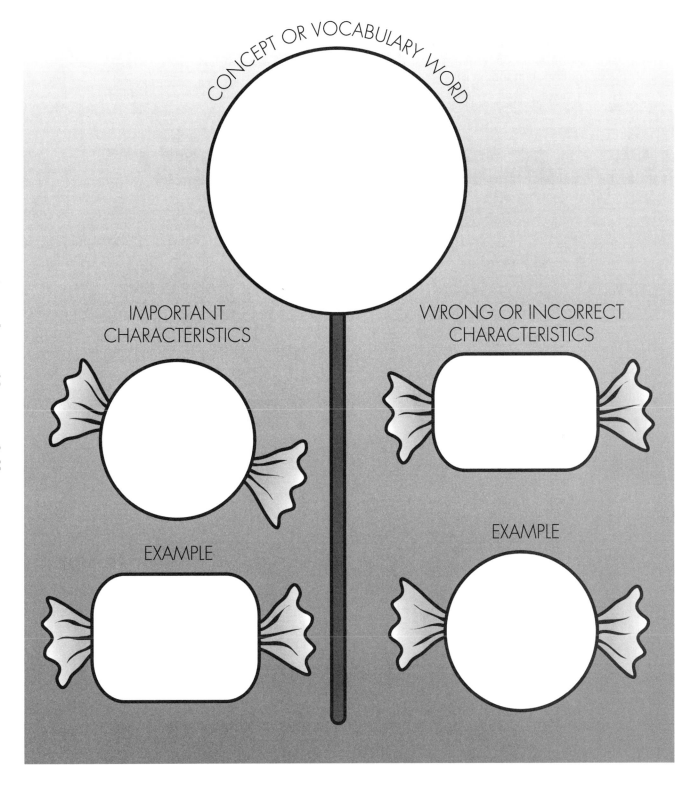

CONCEPT OR VOCABULARY WORD

IMPORTANT CHARACTERISTICS

WRONG OR INCORRECT CHARACTERISTICS

EXAMPLE

EXAMPLE

27 Vocabulary Cluster 1

▶ Grades: 2–5
▶ Level of Difficulty: Medium-Hard

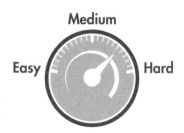

Overview

The Vocabulary Cluster graphic organizer is a visual representation of the connections and associations of a term or word. These connections and associations promote a deeper understanding of a new vocabulary word or concept.

Tips for Classroom Implementation

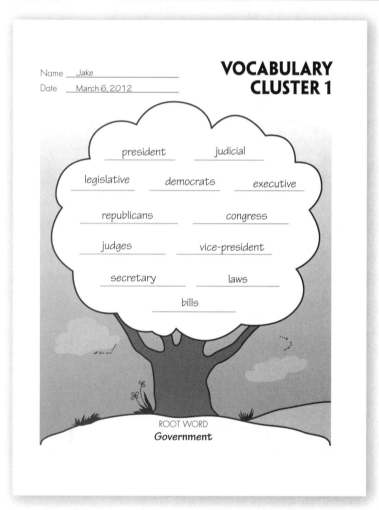

Ask the students to identify the root word and write it at the base of the graphic organizer. Next, either look up or provide the definition for the word or concept to be explored. Prompt the students to provide other examples or synonyms of the word or concept to be explored. Write each synonym or example on the extended parts of the graphic organizer.

It is helpful to write the key word or concept in one color and the examples and synonyms in another color. The students could create this graphic organizer using construction paper.

VOCABULARY
CLUSTER 1

ROOT WORD

28 Vocabulary Cluster 2

▶ Grades: 2–5
▶ Level of Difficulty: Medium-Hard

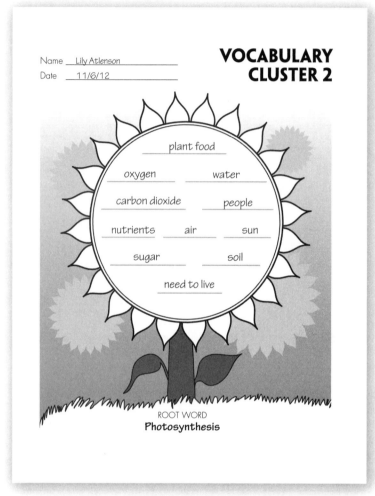

Name _____

Date _____

VOCABULARY CLUSTER 2

ROOT WORD

29 Vocabulary Cluster 3

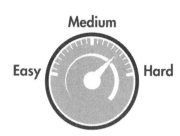

▶ Grades: K–5
▶ Level of Difficulty: Medium-Hard

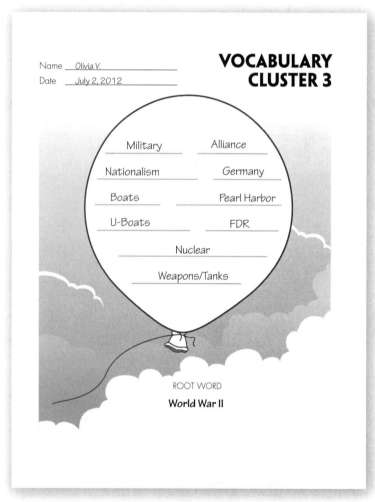

Name _Olivia V._

Date _July 2, 2012_

VOCABULARY CLUSTER 3

Military

Alliance

Nationalism

Germany

Boats

Pearl Harbor

U-Boats

FDR

Nuclear

Weapons/Tanks

ROOT WORD

World War II

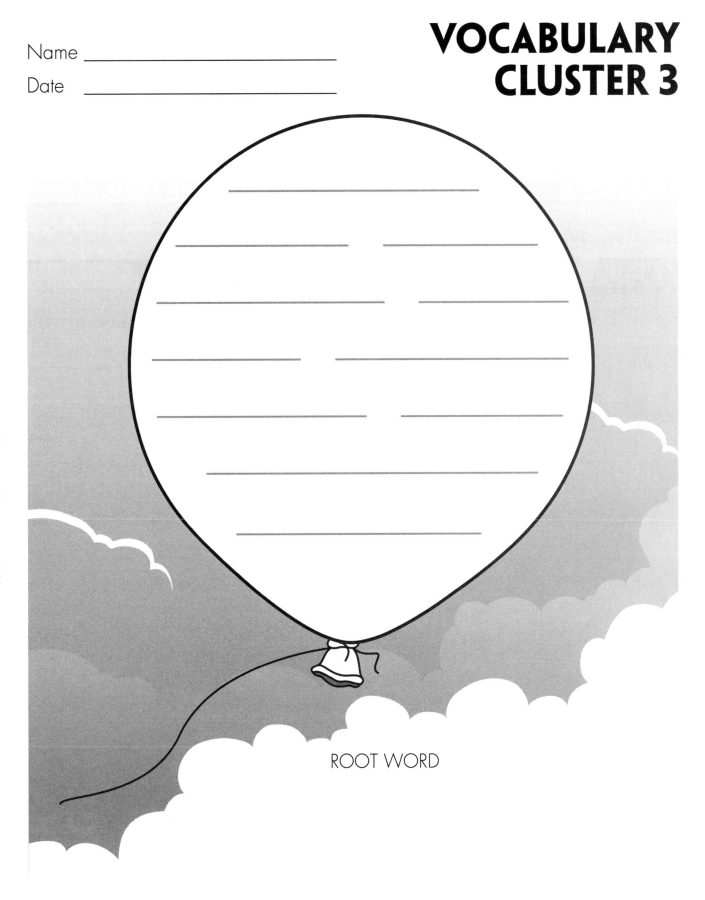

ROOT WORD

30 Word Web

▶ Grades: 2–5
▶ Level of Difficulty: Medium-Hard

Overview

The more ways in which a student uses words, the more likely he or she is to internalize the new vocabulary. The Word Web facilitates student understanding of vocabulary and the relationships of that word.

Tips for Classroom Implementation

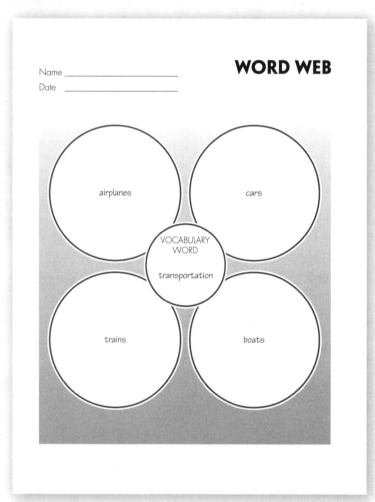

You can model the Word Web for the students as a whole group activity. The vocabulary word should be written in the center circle and the other words that have relationships are written in the surrounding circles.

In addition to using this organizer, you could have the students use different colored markers or pencils to facilitate their understanding of the words and relationships.

WORD WEB

Name _____

Date _____

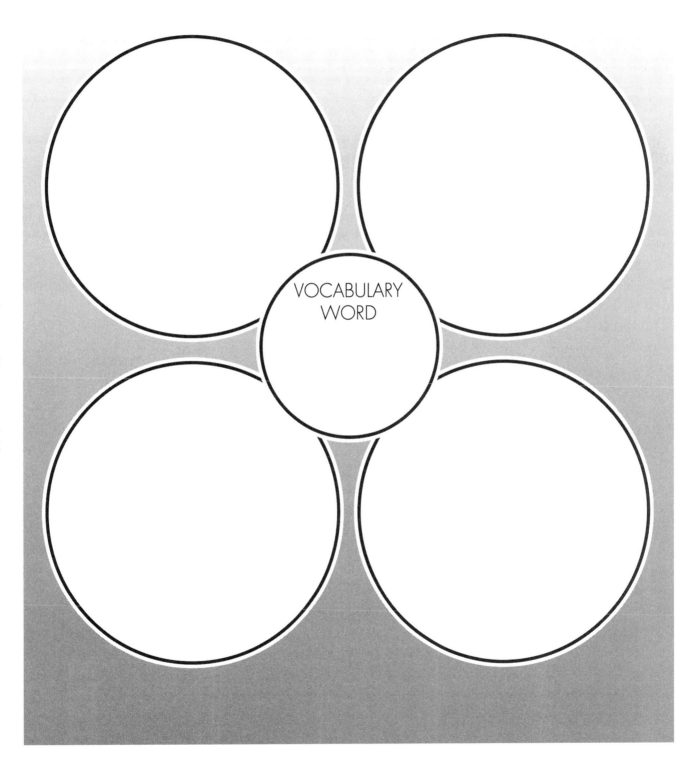

VOCABULARY WORD

31 Dictionary Page

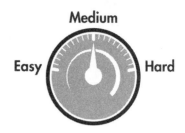

Medium

Easy ——————— Hard

▶ Grades: 2–5
▶ Level of Difficulty: Medium

Overview

This graphic organizer can be used for students to maintain a personal vocabulary list. A personal vocabulary list or dictionary is a useful organizing tool that allows students to keep a list of words that they have learned and need to remember for future study or reference.

Tips for Classroom Implementation

If you are going to use this as a template, make several copies and provide the students with colored paper so that they can make a cover for their personal dictionary. Demonstrate for the students, through a Think Aloud, how you would use this template to record words that you needed to use as reference or to learn. As you go through the Think Aloud with the students, review terms that they may need to know, like "parts of speech."

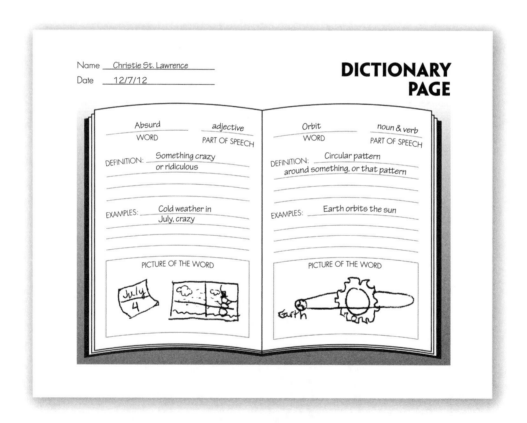

DICTIONARY PAGE

Name _____

Date _____

WORD _____

PART OF SPEECH _____

DEFINITION: _____

EXAMPLES: _____

PICTURE OF THE WORD

WORD _____

PART OF SPEECH _____

DEFINITION: _____

EXAMPLES: _____

PICTURE OF THE WORD

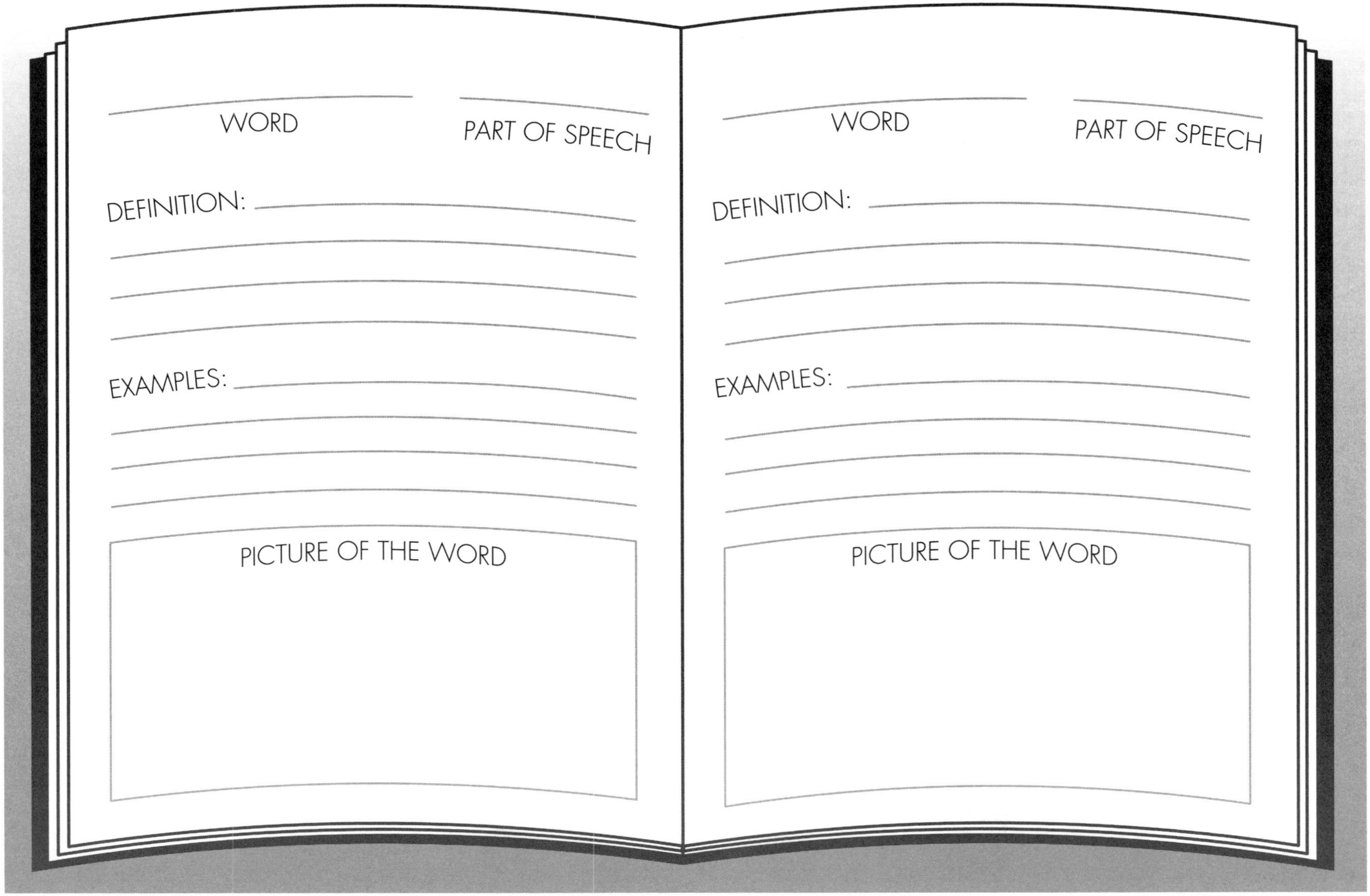

32 Word Chart: Vocabulary Organizer

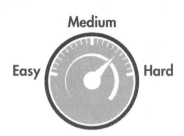

► Grades: 2–5
► Level of Difficulty: Medium-Hard

Overview

The Word Chart is a learning log that allows students to catalog the characteristics of vocabulary words they encounter in their reading or during a unit of study.

Tips for Classroom Implementation

Students can use these organizers as a template for a vocabulary learning log. Each Word Chart can be used in a classroom instruction for students to keep a running record of the vocabulary that they encounter and learn.

Of all of the vocabulary organizers, I probably use Word Charts the most frequently. These are especially useful for keeping a log or history of vocabulary words from a particular unit or chapter.

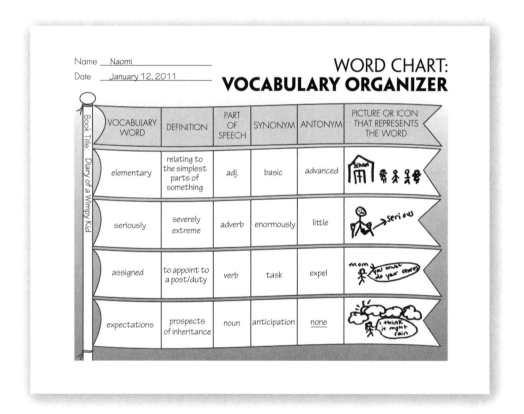

Name _____

Date _____

WORD CHART:
VOCABULARY ORGANIZER

VOCABULARY WORD	DEFINITION	PART OF SPEECH	SYNONYM	ANTONYM	PICTURE OR ICON THAT REPRESENTS THE WORD

Book Title: _____

33   Word Chart: Context Connections

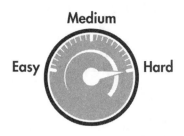

Medium

Easy   Hard

▶ Grades: 2–5
▶ Level of Difficulty: Hard

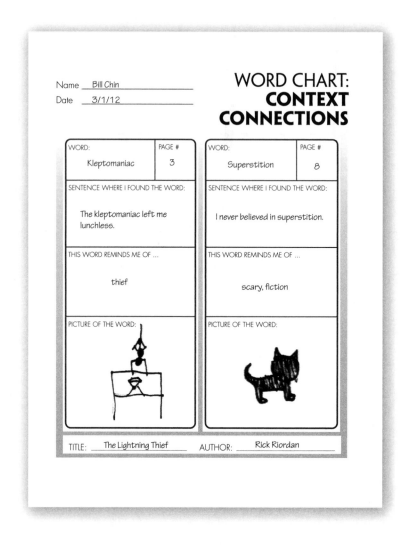

Name ___Bill Chin_____
Date ___3/1/12_____

WORD CHART:
CONTEXT
CONNECTIONS

WORD:	PAGE #
Kleptomaniac	3

SENTENCE WHERE I FOUND THE WORD:

The kleptomaniac left me lunchless.

THIS WORD REMINDS ME OF …

thief

PICTURE OF THE WORD:

WORD:	PAGE #
Superstition	8

SENTENCE WHERE I FOUND THE WORD:

I never believed in superstition.

THIS WORD REMINDS ME OF …

scary, fiction

PICTURE OF THE WORD:

TITLE: ___The Lightning Thief___   AUTHOR: ___Rick Riordan___

Name _____

Date _____

WORD CHART:
CONTEXT CONNECTIONS

WORD:	PAGE #

SENTENCE WHERE I FOUND THE WORD:

THIS WORD REMINDS ME OF …

PICTURE OF THE WORD:

WORD:	PAGE #

SENTENCE WHERE I FOUND THE WORD:

THIS WORD REMINDS ME OF …

PICTURE OF THE WORD:

TITLE: _____   AUTHOR: _____

34   Word Chart: Characteristics and Illustrations

Medium

Easy   Hard

▶ Grades: 2–5
▶ Level of Difficulty: Medium

Name _____

Date _____

WORD CHART:
CHARACTERISTICS
AND ILLUSTRATIONS

WORD:	WORD:	WORD:
PAGE #	PAGE #	PAGE #
PICTURES OF THE WORD:	PICTURES OF THE WORD:	PICTURES OF THE WORD:
MY ILLUSTRATION:	MY ILLUSTRATION:	MY ILLUSTRATION:

35 Vocabulary Tree

▶ Grades: K–5
▶ Level of Difficulty: Easy

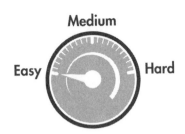

Overview

This highly visual organizer requires students to specify a root word and related words, a strategy that supports students in learning and understanding new vocabulary.

 Tips for Classroom Implementation

In addition to using this graphic organizer as a means to show how words can relate to a root word, I have also used this graphic organizer for writing. The students can use the main trunk for the writing focus and the upper spaces to list details and evidence.

Name _____

Date _____

VOCABULARY TREE

Word

36 Vocabulary Bookmark

▶ Grades: 2–5
▶ Level of Difficulty: Easy

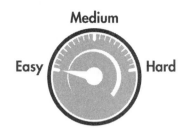

Overview

I have always found Vocabulary Bookmarks to be particularly helpful for students. Bookmarks allow students to create a reference for new words as they are reading. This makes students more active readers and also provides an easily accessible reference so that students can better learn and remember the new vocabulary.

Tips for Classroom Implementation

Each bookmark has space to record four words. Students should write down words that they don't know or are newly encountered. The students can also record the page numbers and additional notes on the bookmark.

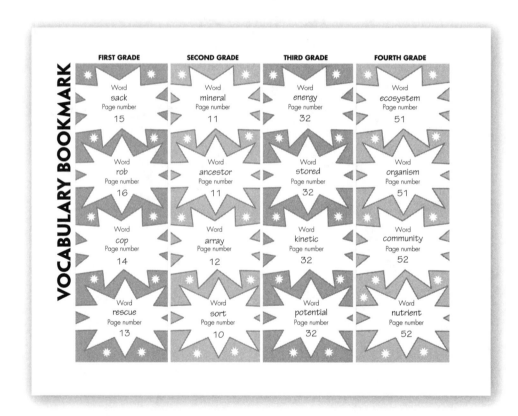

VOCABULARY BOOKMARK

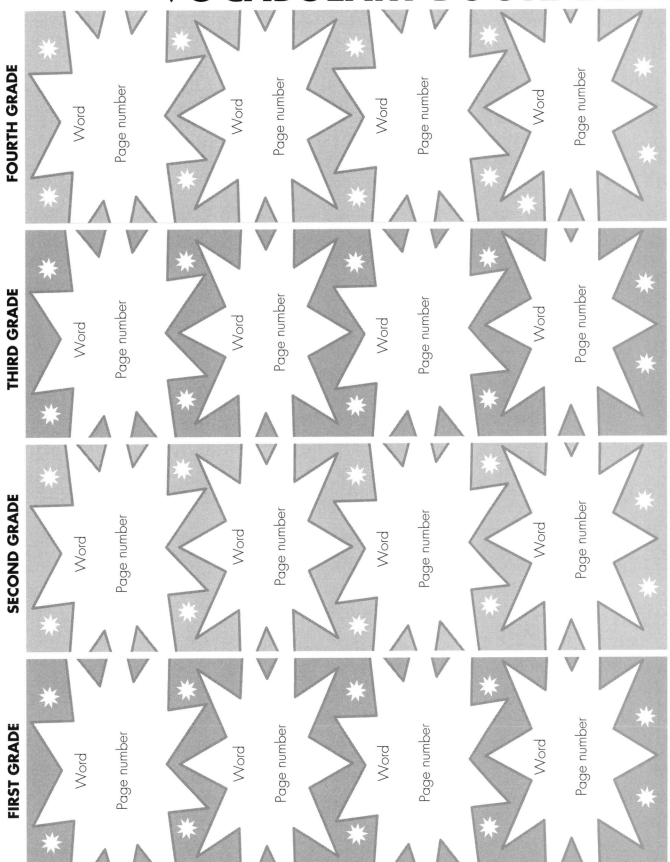

FOURTH GRADE

Word

Page number

Word

Page number

Word

Page number

Word

Page number

THIRD GRADE

Word

Page number

Word

Page number

Word

Page number

Word

Page number

SECOND GRADE

Word

Page number

Word

Page number

Word

Page number

Word

Page number

FIRST GRADE

Word

Page number

Word

Page number

Word

Page number

Word

Page number

CHAPTER FOUR

Graphic Organizers for Note Taking and Study Skills

37 3-Column Notes

► Grades: 2–5
► Level of Difficulty: Medium

Overview

Three-Column Notes are a common graphic organizer structure that can be used in many different formats. KWL is probably one of the best-known three-column graphic organizers.

Tips for Classroom Implementation

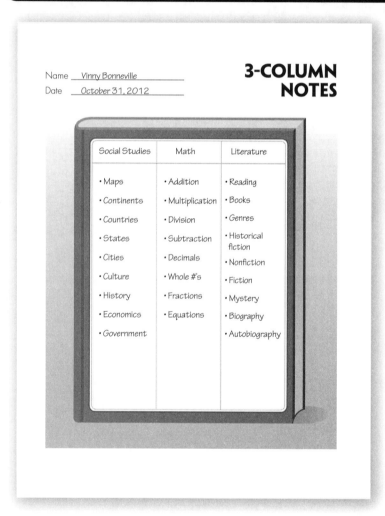

Name   Vinny Bonneville
Date   October 31, 2012

3-COLUMN NOTES

Social Studies	Math	Literature
• Maps	• Addition	• Reading
• Continents	• Multiplication	• Books
• Countries	• Division	• Genres
• States	• Subtraction	• Historical fiction
• Cities	• Decimals	• Nonfiction
• Culture	• Whole #'s	• Fiction
• History	• Fractions	• Mystery
• Economics	• Equations	• Biography
• Government		• Autobiography

For this three-column graphic organizer, the headers are deliberately left blank so that you or the students can create the headers. For younger students, you would probably provide the headers. More advanced students can identify the headers themselves.

Name _____

Date _____

3-COLUMN NOTES

38 T Chart

▶ Grades: K–5
▶ Level of Difficulty: Medium

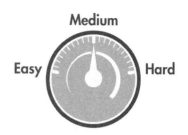
Easy   Medium   Hard

Overview

The T Chart is a graphic organizer that facilitates the students' ability to organize and compare ideas and concepts. In each column, the students record associated ideas and concepts that allow them to begin to develop a language of comparison for these ideas and concepts. The students will also learn how to extend ideas and information on each side of the graphic organizer. The T Chart is an effective structure for students to use to compare and contrast.

Tips for Classroom Implementation

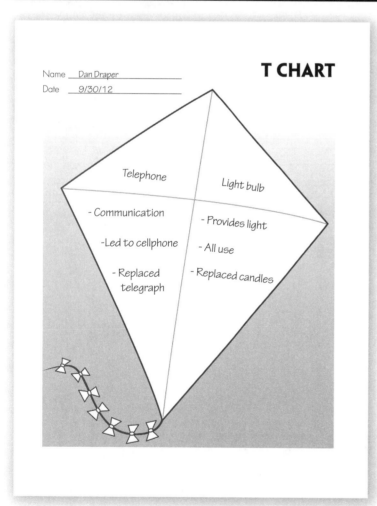

Name   Dan Draper
Date   9/30/12

T CHART

Telephone

Light bulb

- Communication

- Provides light

- Led to cellphone

- All use

- Replaced telegraph

- Replaced candles

Model the T Chart for the students as part of group instruction. Using different colored markers or pens for each area of the graphic organizer is an effective way to emphasize the different kinds of information.

Name _____

Date _____

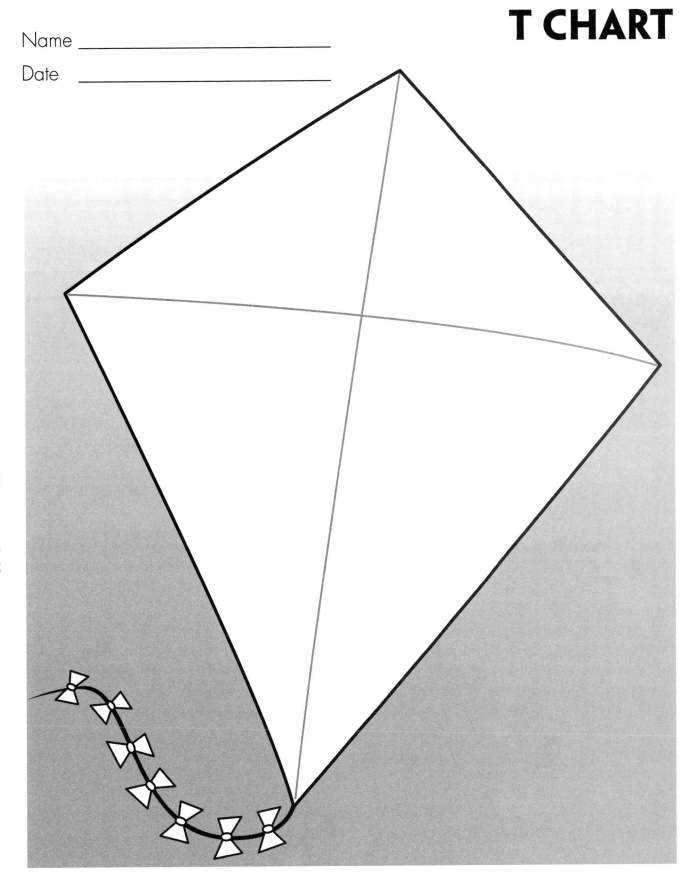

39 Scientific Method

▶ Grades: 2–5
▶ Level of Difficulty: Hard

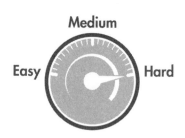

Overview

This graphic organizer is designed to guide students through the scientific method. Teaching the students the process of the scientific method so that they formulate a question (hypothesis) reinforces important ideas and concepts. Once the students create a question, they can test and evaluate it. As always, it is beneficial to model the graphic organizer for the students.

Tips for Classroom Implementation

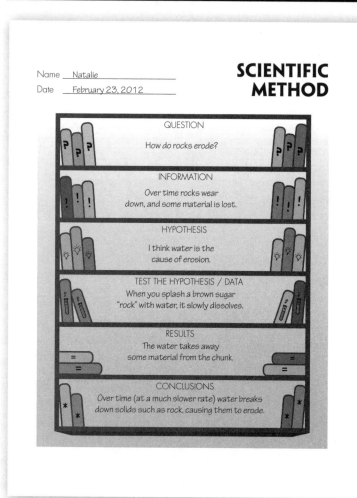

A scientific experiment may comprise the following:

1. When you observe something, you may have questions about that phenomenon. State your QUESTION.
2. Gather as much INFORMATION as you can about your question.
3. Find out what information has already been discovered about your question.
4. Formulate a HYPOTHESIS. Write a statement that predicts what may happen in your experiment.
5. Design an experiment to test your hypothesis.
6. Perform the experiment.
7. Collect DATA. Record the results of the investigation.
8. Summarize RESULTS. Analyze the data and note trends in your experimental results.
9. Draw CONCLUSIONS. Determine whether or not the data support the hypothesis of your experiment.

Name _____

Date _____

SCIENTIFIC METHOD

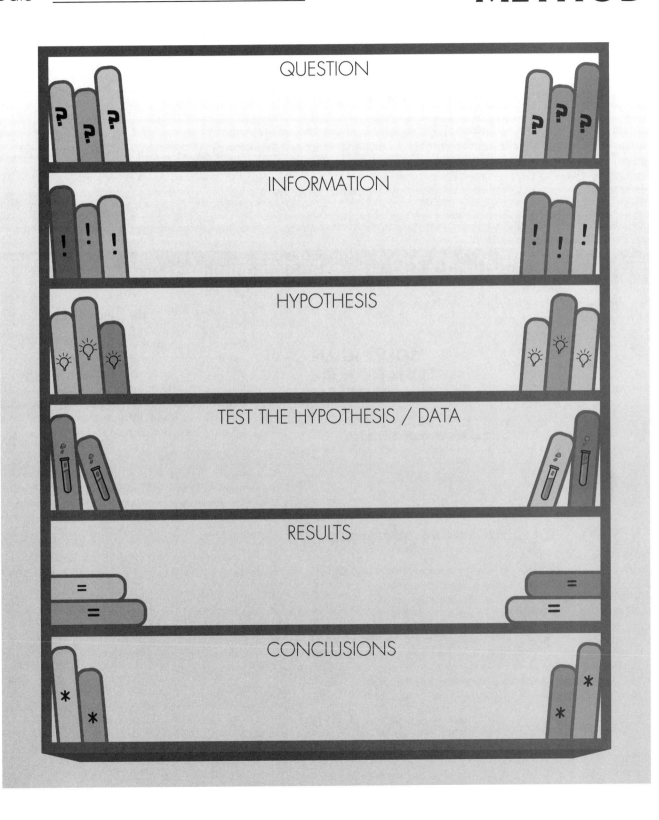

QUESTION

INFORMATION

HYPOTHESIS

TEST THE HYPOTHESIS / DATA

RESULTS

CONCLUSIONS

40 Solving an Equation or Problem

► Grades: 2–5
► Level of Difficulty: Hard

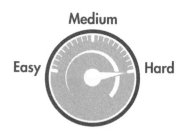

Overview

When students are given the opportunity to break down (or chunk) and visualize what they are learning, it supports understanding and comprehension. This equation/problem graphic organizer facilitates this process. The three spaces—the problem or question, the approach to solving the problem, and the solution—break down the information into more digestible chunks for students. For each space, I advise that students create a picture or visualization of the problem that they are breaking down.

Tips for Classroom Implementation

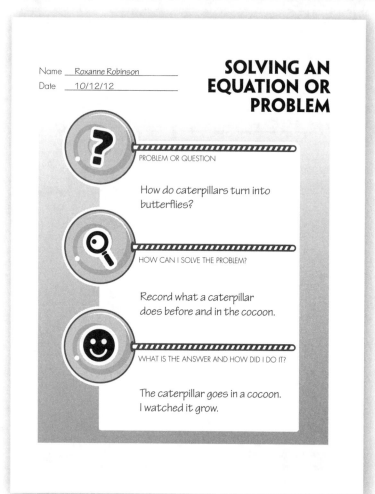

Model for the students how to break down the steps for solving a problem or question: the problem or question, the approach to solving the problem, and the solution. Use words and pictures (pictures are especially useful for nonreaders and beginning readers). Take students through each step. You may also want to consider using different colored markers for each step and corresponding blank.

Name _____

Date _____

SOLVING AN EQUATION OR PROBLEM

PROBLEM OR QUESTION

HOW CAN I SOLVE THE PROBLEM?

WHAT IS THE ANSWER AND HOW DID I DO IT?

41 Food Chain Organizer

▶ Grades: 2–5
▶ Level of Difficulty: Medium

Overview

Sequencing and understanding a chain of events is an important learning skill for students to develop. This graphic organizer prompts students to identify important and critical information in a sequence or chain of events. It has several applications, which include charting a story plot, illustrating a scientific sequence, identifying the steps for a math problem, and identifying important elements in a text or event.

Tips for Classroom Implementation

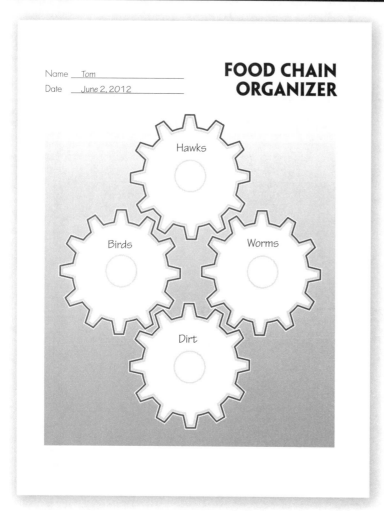

Model the graphic organizer as a Think Aloud for the students. It is always helpful to use different colored markers or pens so that the students can more easily chunk and organize the information.

Name _____

Date _____

FOOD CHAIN ORGANIZER

42 Fact or Opinion

▶ Grades: 2–5
▶ Level of Difficulty: Medium

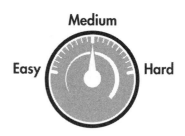

Overview

Students are often challenged when they need to determine whether a statement is a fact or an opinion. Discerning the difference requires students to closely examine subtleties and inferences that can support them to identify facts and opinions. This two-column organizer graphically organizes facts and opinions for students.

Tips for Classroom Implementation

This graphic organizer is particularly useful when the students are identifying key information from a text. The students harvest the important details and then identify whether each is a fact or opinion. Using different colored pens or markers for the facts and opinions also helps students to understand and comprehend the material.

Name _____

Date _____

FACT OR OPINION

FACTS

OPINIONS

43 Prediction Chart

▶ Grades: K–5
▶ Level of Difficulty: Medium

Overview

The Prediction Chart is a two-column graphic organizer that supports students to further their comprehension and understanding. When students are able to take information and then generate further ideas and thoughts, they develop ideas that go beyond basic understanding. Prediction is an important skill for active and engaged readers. In contrast, struggling and less independent readers rarely make predictions about what they are reading or studying.

Tips for Classroom Implementation

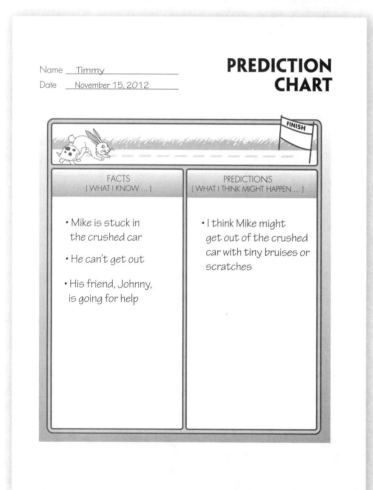

Through a Think Aloud, complete the left-hand side of the graphic organizer, listing the facts and main ideas from a text or what the students might be studying. For the right-hand column, be sure to explain what a prediction is—what we think might happen—and compose several predictions. For this kind of graphic organizer, it is always helpful to use different colored markers or pens for the facts and predictions columns.

Name _____

Date _____

PREDICTION CHART

FACTS (WHAT I KNOW ...)	PREDICTIONS (WHAT I THINK MIGHT HAPPEN ...)

44 Questions: Book Notes

▶ Grades: 2–5
▶ Level of Difficulty: Medium

Overview

This graphic organizer should be used as a bookmark as means to promote active reading for students. The questions can help guide the students as they go through the text.

Tips for Classroom Implementation

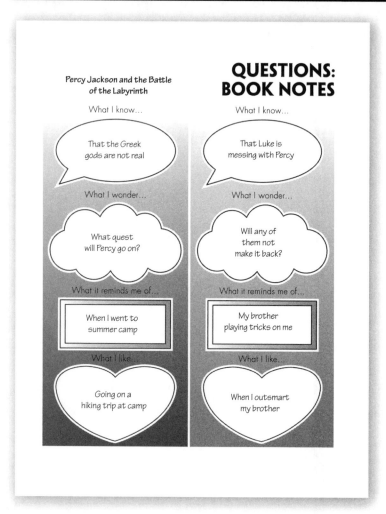

Younger students can use the bookmark as a guide. In grades 2–5 the students can use the bookmark to record their questions, comments, and predictions as they read. There are two bookmarks that can be cut out on the page for duplication.

QUESTIONS: BOOK NOTES

What I know…

What I know…

What I wonder…

What I wonder…

What it reminds me of…

What it reminds me of…

What I like…

What I like…

45 Term (In My Words) Picture

▶ Grades: 2–5
▶ Level of Difficulty: Medium

Overview

Active readers who comprehend are able to visualize text. This graphic organizer and activity supports students in becoming able to represent what they understand with pictures. It is important to note that the latest literacy research indicates that the more details depicted in a picture or visual representation, the greater the comprehension.

Tips for Classroom Implementation

Explain to students that good readers have pictures in their head when they are reading a text. The pictures help us to understand what we are learning and reading. For this graphic organizer, explain to the students that they are going to take an important word or term from the text and illustrate it.

Name _____

Date _____

46 Student Self-Assessment

▶ Grades: 2–5
▶ Level of Difficulty: Easy

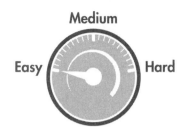

Overview

This graphic organizer encourages students to reflect on their learning and to evaluate their individual performance in a cooperative group. It draws attention to their role in the success of that group in completing an assigned task.

 Tips for Classroom Implementation

Model and coach the students—especially younger students—through the self-assessment before they complete it independently.

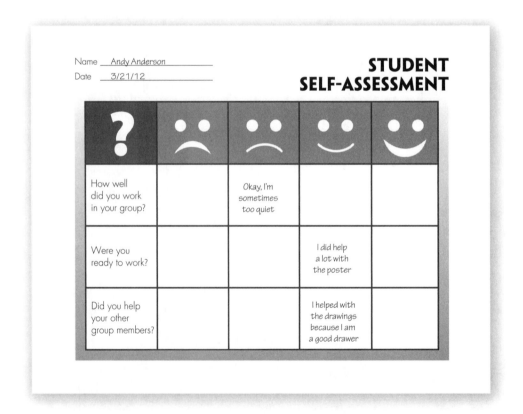

Name ___Andy Anderson___
Date ___3/21/12___

STUDENT SELF-ASSESSMENT

?	😕	🙁	🙂	😀
How well did you work in your group?		Okay, I'm sometimes too quiet		
Were you ready to work?			I did help a lot with the poster	
Did you help your other group members?			I helped with the drawings because I am a good drawer	

STUDENT
SELF-ASSESSMENT

Name _____

Date _____

？	🙁	🙂	😊	😄
How well did you work in your group?				
Were you ready to work?				
Did you help your other group members?				

47 My Portfolio

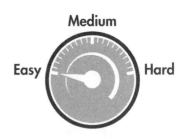

▶ Grades: 2–5
▶ Level of Difficulty: Easy

Overview

Portfolios are designed to demonstrate and showcase the development of a student's knowledge and skills. Portfolios can be a substantive and rewarding form of assessment. Part of the effectiveness of portfolios is that students must actively participate in keeping track of the contents.

Tips for Classroom Implementation

When you introduce portfolios to your students, explain that they are vehicles for students to document their journeys as learners. A portfolio should contain examples of each student's best work. The teacher and student work together to decide what should be part of the portfolio.

MY PORTFOLIO

Name _____

Date _____

COMPLETION DATE

TITLE OF WORK

WHY WAS THIS WORK SELECTED?

48 Homework Organizer

▶ Grades: 2–5
▶ Level of Difficulty: Easy

Overview

Many students benefit from support structures so that they can effectively manage short- and long-term assignments. This graphic organizer helps students to record and track their homework assignments.

Tips for Classroom Implementation

Providing students with completed Homework Organizer samples serves as a helpful model for the students. You may want to consider making large copies of the accompanying student sample.

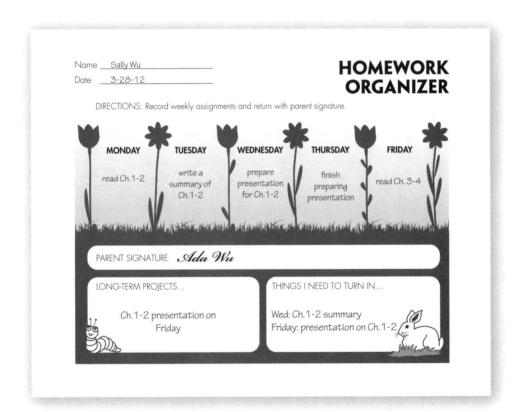

Name _____

Date _____

HOMEWORK ORGANIZER

DIRECTIONS: Record weekly assignments and return with parent signature.

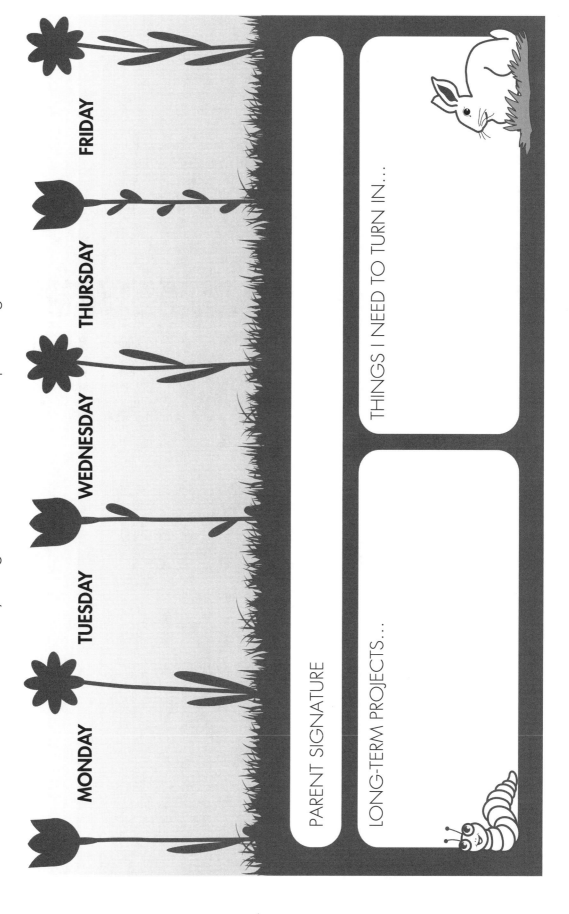

MONDAY

TUESDAY

WEDNESDAY

THURSDAY

FRIDAY

PARENT SIGNATURE

LONG-TERM PROJECTS...

THINGS I NEED TO TURN IN...

49 Group Learning

▶ Grades: 3–5
▶ Level of Difficulty: Easy

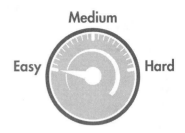

Overview

This graphic organizer reminds students of the actions and qualities that are needed for successful group work. Students need to learn how to work in cooperative learning groups. Breaking down the skills and attitudes needed in order to successfully implement this is foundational to this learning structure.

Tips for Classroom Implementation

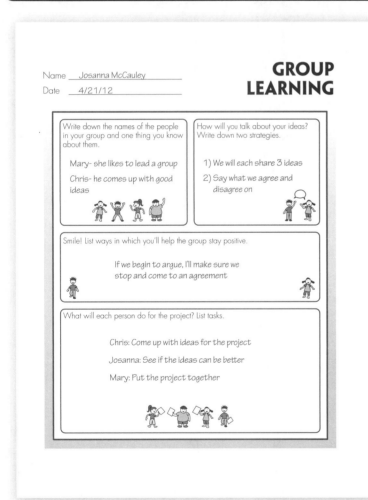

Learning how to successfully participate in cooperative learning groups is an important skill set for students to develop. Modeling and role playing effective cooperative learning groups helps students to learn these necessary skills.

Name _____

Date _____

GROUP LEARNING

Write down the names of the people in your group and one thing you know about them.

How will you talk about your ideas? Write down two strategies.

Smile! List ways in which you'll help the group stay positive.

What will each person do for the project? List tasks.

50 Oral Reports Organizer

▶ Grades: 3–5
▶ Level of Difficulty: Medium

Overview

Developing a great question, learning how to find information to answer the question and then sharing the information—these are skills we use throughout school and our careers. Developing these skills helps students to ask questions about their world, understand their world, and share insights and responses to their understanding of their world. These are complex skills, so it is important that we break down or scaffold these steps for our students.

Tips for Classroom Implementation

I cannot overly stress how important it is to model great questions for students. So many of our students are rarely given the opportunity to pose and answer their own questions. Model how to develop questions and also how to find information to answer student questions.

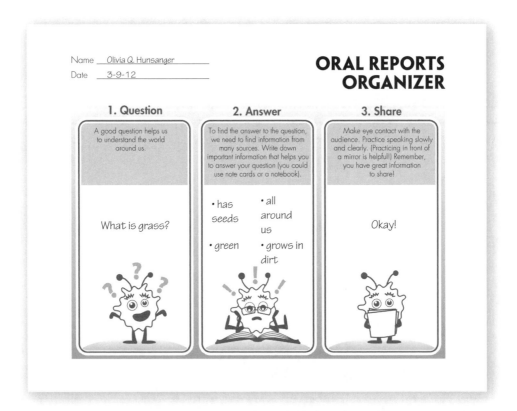

Name _____

Date _____

ORAL REPORTS ORGANIZER

1. Question

A good question helps us to understand the world around us.

2. Answer

To find the answer to the question, we need to find information from many sources. Write down important information that helps you to answer your question (you could use note cards or a notebook).

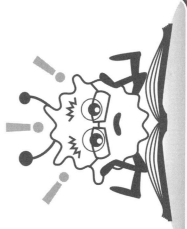

3. Share

Make eye contact with the audience. Practice speaking slowly and clearly. (Practicing in front of a mirror is helpful!) Remember, you have great information to share!

51 Interviewing Organizer

▶ Grades: 3–5
▶ Level of Difficulty: Medium

Overview

When we interview a person, we usually pose who, what, where, when, and how questions. These questions are essential in gathering information and allowing interviewers to discover important details so that they can present this information in oral or written form.

Tips for Classroom Implementation

You will need to model this graphic organizer for your students. After the students have completed the organizer, you will need to ask them some additional questions to further deepen the gathered information. Model questions like these:

What do you know about this person?
Why is this information important?

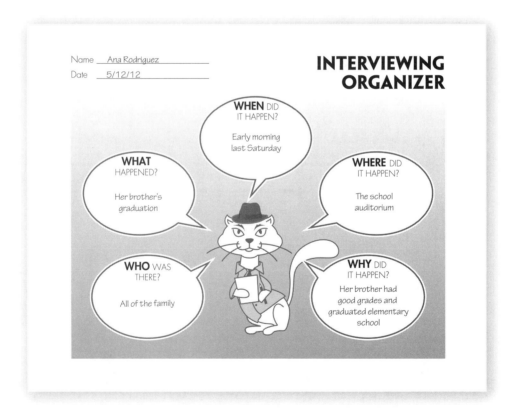

INTERVIEWING ORGANIZER

Name _____

Date _____

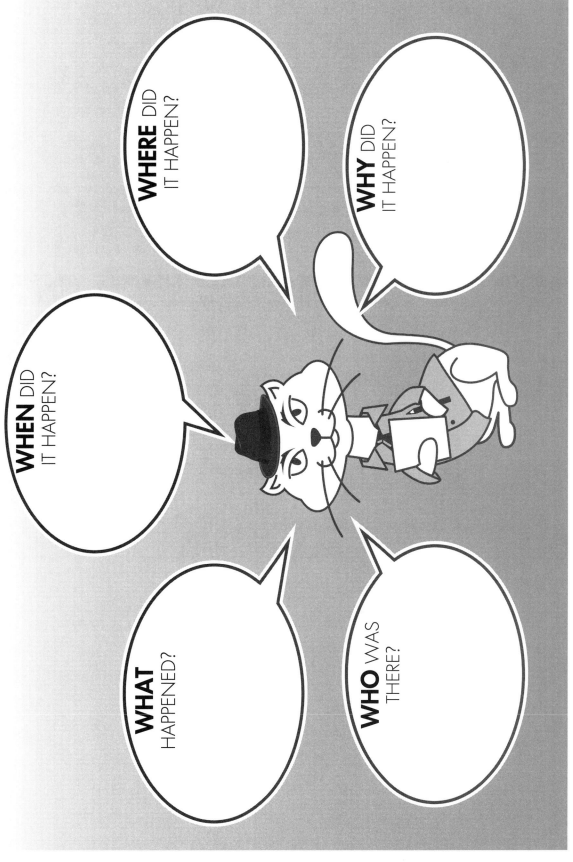

WHERE DID IT HAPPEN?

WHY DID IT HAPPEN?

WHEN DID IT HAPPEN?

WHAT HAPPENED?

WHO WAS THERE?

52 Reading Recorder/Organizer

▶ Grades: 3–5
▶ Level of Difficulty: Medium

Overview

We want students to become active, engaged, and thoughtful readers. When readers are in an active stance, it leads to greater comprehension and understanding of the text. This graphic organizer prompts students to record what they understand about a text at the simple recall level and then prompts them to go beyond their basic understanding to a more reflective and predictive stance.

Tips for Classroom Implementation

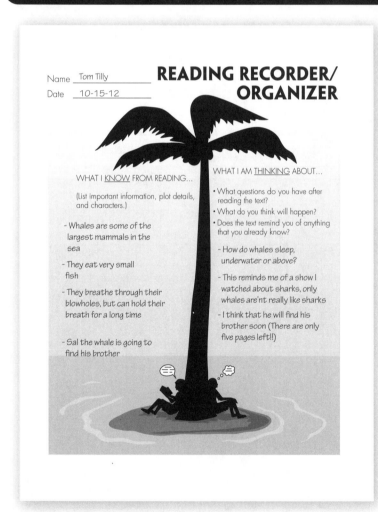

Model this graphic organizer through a Read Aloud with the students. Again, in a Read Aloud, you read from a mentor text—that is, a different text from the one the students are reading—and model how to record what you recall from the text, in the first column. You will continue to explore your understanding in the second column as you model your reflections, insights, predictions, and questions.

Name _____

Date _____

READING RECORDER/ ORGANIZER

WHAT I <u>KNOW</u> FROM READING…

(List important information, plot details, and characters.)

WHAT I AM <u>THINKING</u> ABOUT…

- What questions do you have after reading the text?
- What do you think will happen?
- Does the text remind you of anything that you already know?

CHAPTER FIVE

Graphic Organizers for Literacy

53 RAFT Papers

▶ Grades: 3–5
▶ Level of Difficulty: Medium-Hard

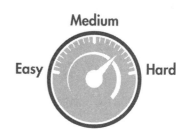

Overview

RAFT stands for *role*, *audience*, *format*, and *topic*. This organizer helps students plan for successful writing.

Tips for Classroom Implementation

Explain each of the organizer elements.

Role: Students can take on any role they like, such as that of a scientist or a specific historical figure.

Audience: This could be another author, the U.S. Congress, or any real or imaginary group.

Format: Students can choose any format. Here are some suggestions: journal or diary, letter, play, newspaper article, science fiction, fantasy.

Topic: Students briefly describe what they will write about.

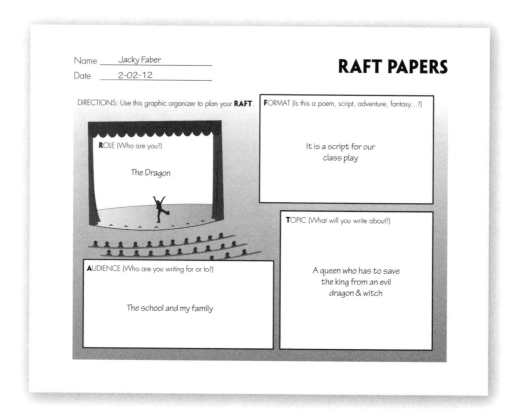

Name _____

Date _____

RAFT PAPERS

DIRECTIONS: Use this graphic organizer to plan your **RAFT**.

FORMAT (Is this a poem, script, adventure, fantasy...?)

TOPIC (What will you write about?)

ROLE (Who are you?)

AUDIENCE (Who are you writing for or to?)

54 Story Trails

► Grades: K–5
► Level of Difficulty: Medium-Hard

Easy — Medium — Hard

Overview

Students will develop the following reading strategies for this kind of graphic organizer:

Making personal connections
Using prior knowledge
Predicting
Visualizing
Making inferences

This graphic organizer offers a structure for students to use to put events from a story or the stages of an historical event into chronological order. Understanding of the key events facilitates greater exploration into the structure of the story.

Are the events related by cause and effect, do they connect as situation-problem-solution, or is the story simply one of beginning-middle-end? Recording the text and visual images of the key events also enhances students' comprehension.

Tips for Classroom Implementation

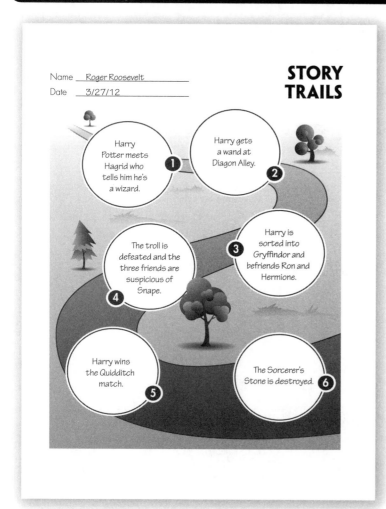

When you first introduce students to Story Trails and History Maps (Graphic Organizer 55), select the key events, arrange them in chronological order, and instruct the students to reexamine these events for specific details that can be illustrated.

Name _____

Date _____

1

2

3

4

5

6

55 History Map

▶ Grades: K–5
▶ Level of Difficulty: Easy-Medium-Hard

Easy   Hard

The History Map graphic organizer is similar to Graphic Organizer 54, Story Trails. See the overview and tips for classroom implementation for that graphic organizer.

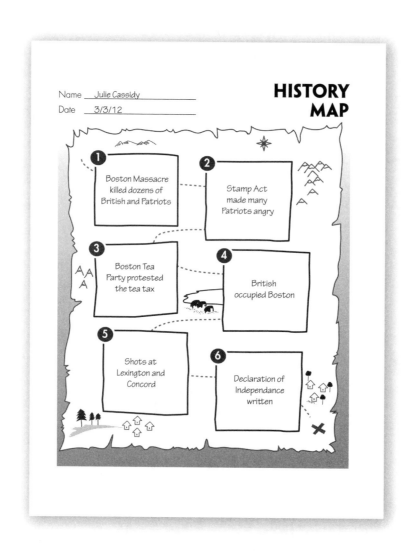

Name _____

Date _____

HISTORY MAP

1

2

3

4

5

6

56 Inquiry Chart

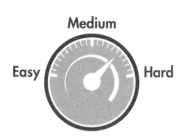

▶ Grades: 3–5
▶ Level of Difficulty: Medium-Hard

Overview

An Inquiry Chart prompts students to record what they already know about a particular topic.

Tips for Classroom Implementation

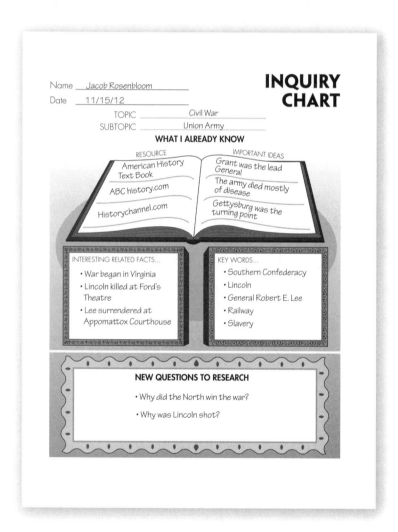

Inquiry Charts can be used individually, in small cooperative learning groups, or with the whole class. Students list their topic and any information that they already know about the topic. Next, they consult resources and note bibliographic information.

The limited amount of note-taking space is deliberate. It encourages students to selectively summarize important information. There is space on the organizer to record key words and questions that students might have while conducting their research.

INQUIRY CHART

Name ______________________

Date ______________________

TOPIC ______________________

SUBTOPIC ______________________

WHAT I ALREADY KNOW

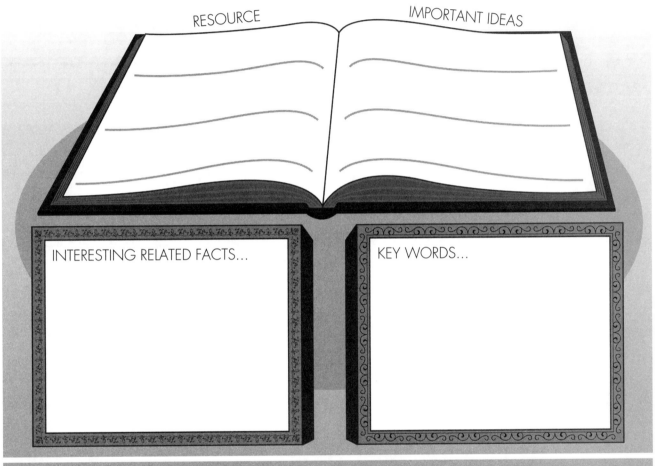

RESOURCE

IMPORTANT IDEAS

INTERESTING RELATED FACTS...

KEY WORDS...

NEW QUESTIONS TO RESEARCH

Copyright © 2013 by John Wiley & Sons, Inc.

57   Story Map 1

▶ Grades: K–5
▶ Level of Difficulty: Easy

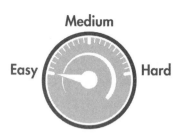

Overview

This graphic organizer helps students prepare and organize ideas and details for a story.

Tips for Classroom Implementation

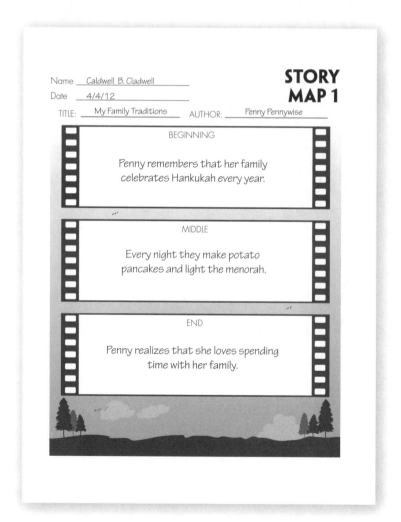

Review with students the basic elements of story structure. For younger students, remind them that stories always have a beginning, middle, and end. For older students, effective stories always have a situation, problem, and solution.

In a Think Aloud, give each student one of the blank Story Map organizers and model how to complete it. You can discuss the main story elements: setting, plot, theme, and characters. As the students read, they can complete the Story Map. This can also be used as a center or as a during-reading or after-reading activity. Because there are three versions of the Story Map graphic organizer, you can differentiate the activity for your students by giving them different organizers based on student levels.

Story Maps are also useful in mathematics as an organizer for solving word or story problems.

Name _____

Date _____

TITLE: _____ AUTHOR: _____

BEGINNING

MIDDLE

END

58 Story Map 2

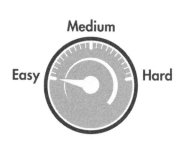

Medium

Easy | Hard

▶ Grades: K–5
▶ Level of Difficulty: Easy

See the description for Graphic Organizer 57.

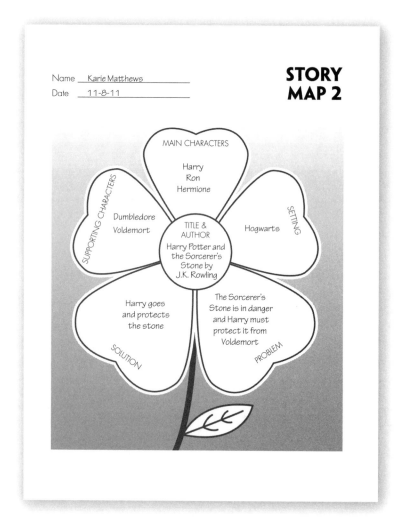

Name Karie Matthews
Date 11-8-11

STORY MAP 2

MAIN CHARACTERS

Harry
Ron
Hermione

SUPPORTING CHARACTERS

Dumbledore
Voldemort

SETTING

Hogwarts

TITLE &
AUTHOR
Harry Potter and
the Sorcerer's
Stone by
J.K. Rowling

Harry goes
and protects
the stone

The Sorcerer's
Stone is in danger
and Harry must
protect it from
Voldemort

SOLUTION

PROBLEM

Name _____

Date _____

STORY MAP 2

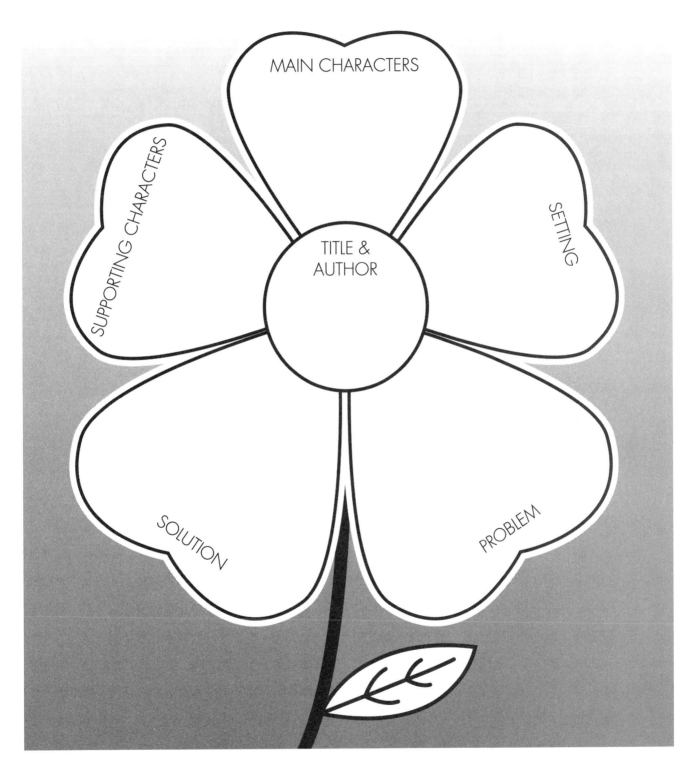

MAIN CHARACTERS

SUPPORTING CHARACTERS

SETTING

TITLE & AUTHOR

SOLUTION

PROBLEM

59 Story Map 3

▶ Grades: 3–5
▶ Level of Difficulty: Hard

See the description for Graphic Organizer 57.

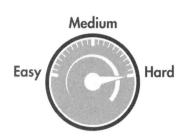

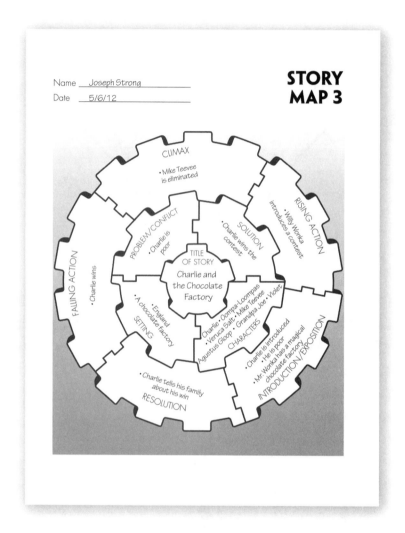

Name _____

Date _____

STORY MAP 3

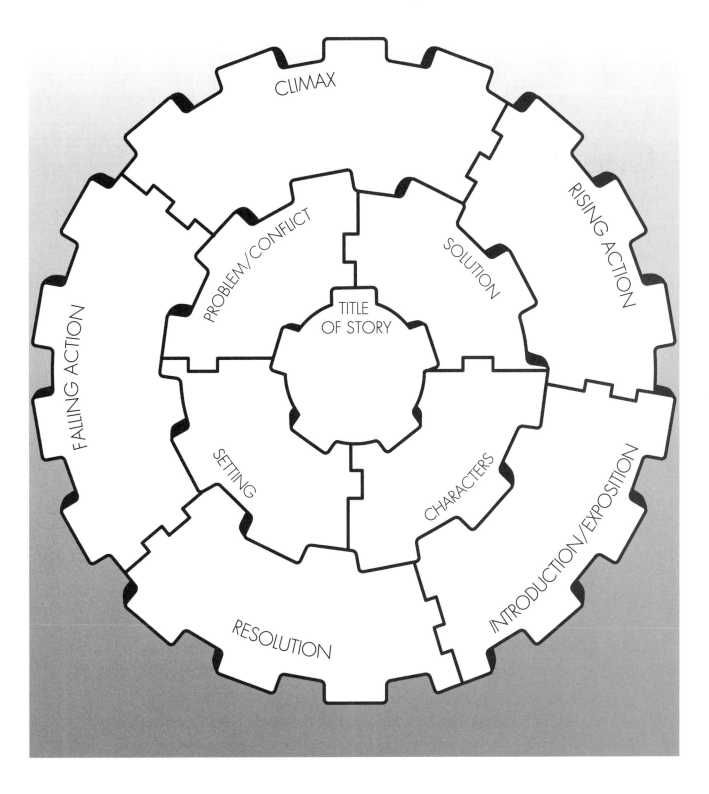

Labels within the diagram:

CLIMAX

RISING ACTION

PROBLEM/CONFLICT

SOLUTION

TITLE OF STORY

FALLING ACTION

SETTING

CHARACTERS

INTRODUCTION/EXPOSITION

RESOLUTION

60 Sequence of Events

► Grades: K–5
► Level of Difficulty: Medium-Hard

Overview

The Sequence of Events graphic organizer is good for placing events in the order of occurrence. This graphic organizer can be used in language arts, social studies, mathematics, and science.

Tips for Classroom Implementation

Sequencing is one of the most important skills in the development of reading comprehension. When students are able to organize events, they are more likely engaged in an active stance for reading and learning. Modeling this graphic organizer through a Think Aloud will help the students to use it independently, possibly in a literacy center. I also suggest that when modeling this graphic organizer you use different colored markers or pens so that the students can see the different events more clearly. This is particularly helpful for students with special needs.

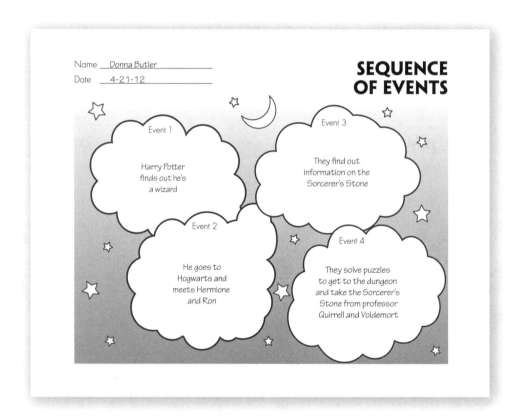

SEQUENCE OF EVENTS

Name _____

Date _____

Event 1

Event 2

Event 3

Event 4

61 Small Book Template

▶ Grades: K–5
▶ Level of Difficulty: Easy-Medium-Hard

Overview

When I taught, I don't know who got more pleasure from creating Small Books, the students or me. I love creating small books on different topics. And when I was a little girl (in the days before the Internet), I remember pulling out volumes of *World Book Encyclopedia* and creating mini-books on subjects that were of personal interest. It's a nerdy activity but one that I still enjoy today with my ten-year-old son.

Mini-books are an effective instructional tool for several reasons:

1. Students enjoy creating a product or artifact of their own learning.
2. Mini-books facilitate summarization. The structure encourages students to edit information down to the most important details and facts.
3. Creating strong visualizations facilitates comprehension and understanding.

Tips for Classroom Implementation

Provide some samples of mini-books for the students. There are tons on different Internet sites in addition to the student samples in this book. This is also a great activity for a literacy or learning center.

Instructions:

1. Cut out the rectangles.
2. Stack the rectangles, largest on the bottom, smallest on the top.
3. Fold in half, then stack, aligning the folds.
4. Staple on the center seam.

STEP ONE: CUT OUT RECTANGLES

STEP TWO: STACK THE RECTANGLES....etc.

STEP THREE: FOLD IN HALF

STEP FOUR: STAPLE ON THE CENTER SEAM

62　Story Pyramid

▶ Grades: 1–5
▶ Level of Difficulty: Medium-Hard

Overview

This graphic organizer helps students organize story components, which makes it a useful prewriting tool. Model it through large group instruction.

Tips for Classroom Implementation

The Story Pyramid graphic organizer is an effective activity for guided reading or literature circles, or as a literacy center once the students have learned how to complete it through modeling. The students can create their Story Pyramid on construction paper, use different colored markers for the different components, and add visuals.

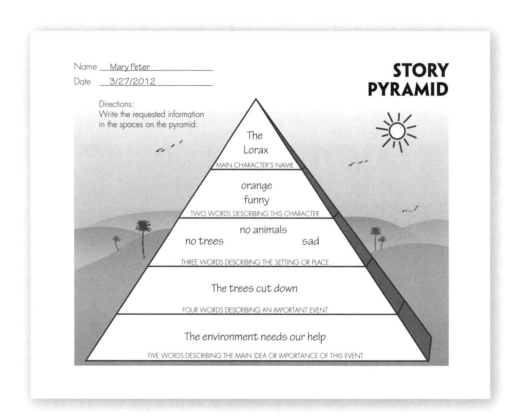

Name Mary Peter

Date 3/27/2012

STORY PYRAMID

Directions:
Write the requested information in the spaces on the pyramid.

The Lorax
MAIN CHARACTER'S NAME

orange
funny
TWO WORDS DESCRIBING THIS CHARACTER

no animals
no trees   sad
THREE WORDS DESCRIBING THE SETTING OR PLACE

The trees cut down
FOUR WORDS DESCRIBING AN IMPORTANT EVENT

The environment needs our help
FIVE WORDS DESCRIBING THE MAIN IDEA OR IMPORTANCE OF THIS EVENT

Name _____

Date _____

STORY PYRAMID

Directions:
Write the requested information
in the spaces on the pyramid.

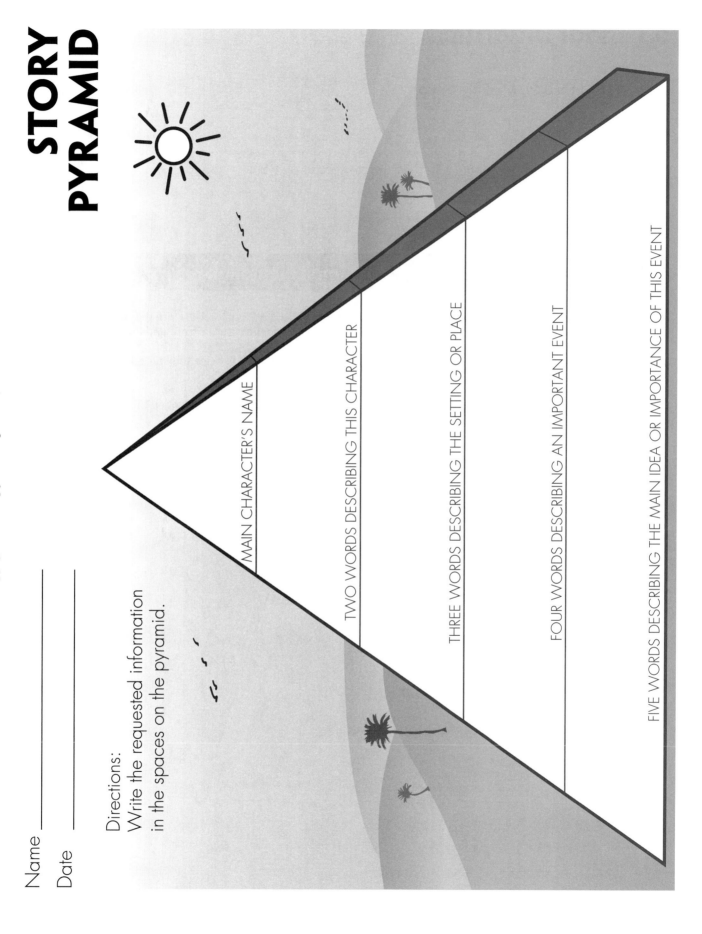

MAIN CHARACTER'S NAME

TWO WORDS DESCRIBING THIS CHARACTER

THREE WORDS DESCRIBING THE SETTING OR PLACE

FOUR WORDS DESCRIBING AN IMPORTANT EVENT

FIVE WORDS DESCRIBING THE MAIN IDEA OR IMPORTANCE OF THIS EVENT

63 Plot Diagram

▶ Grades: 1–5
▶ Level of Difficulty: Medium-Hard

Easy — Medium — Hard

Overview

Plot diagrams help students to organize and sequence important events in a narrative text as well as expose and reinforce the concept of plot as a literary element.

Tips for Classroom Implementation

Model the graphic organizer with the students, using a mentor text through a Think Aloud. Once the students understand how to use the graphic organizer, you can incorporate it in guided reading, literature circles, and literacy centers.

Designating the different plot elements with different colored markers and pens helps the students to distinguish the different plot components.

This Plot Diagram graphic organizer can be challenging. Graphic Organizer 64, What Happen? is more accessible for younger students.

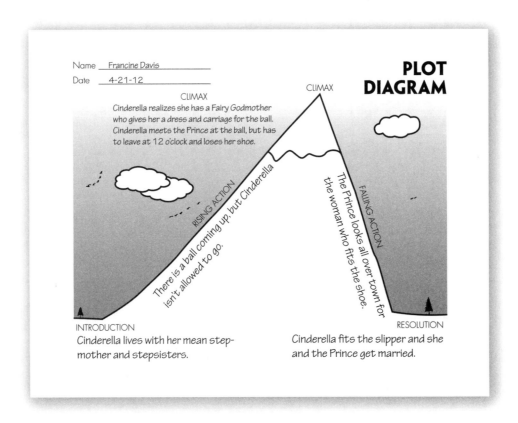

PLOT DIAGRAM

Name _____

Date _____

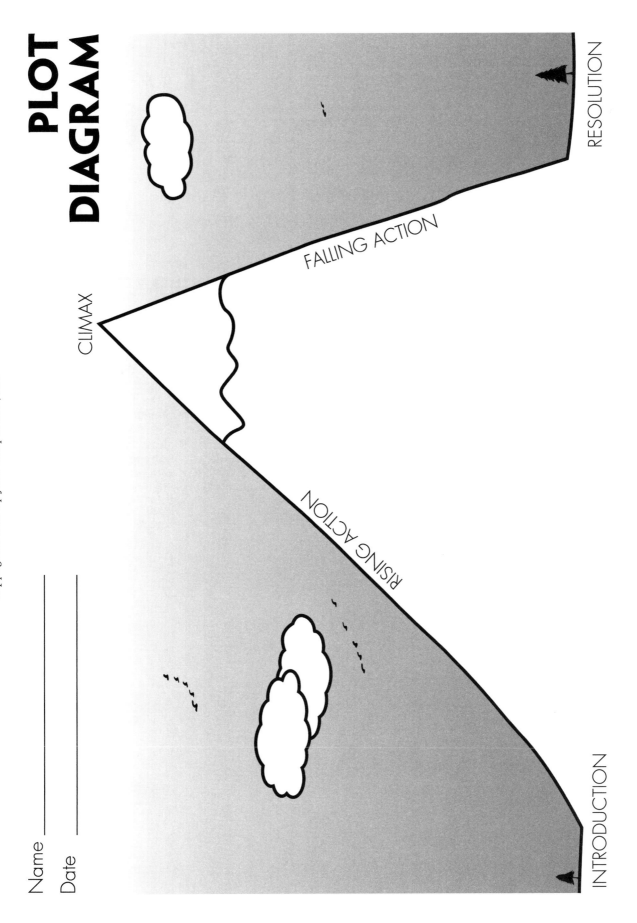

CLIMAX

RISING ACTION

FALLING ACTION

INTRODUCTION

RESOLUTION

64   What Happens?

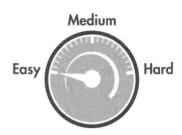

▶ Grades: 2–5
▶ Level of Difficulty: Easy

Overview

This graphic organizer supports students in developing skills in the sequencing of events and summarization. Understanding chronological organization is important for students to understand texts and structures that include history, recipes, directions, procedures, and narrative writing.

Tips for Classroom Implementation

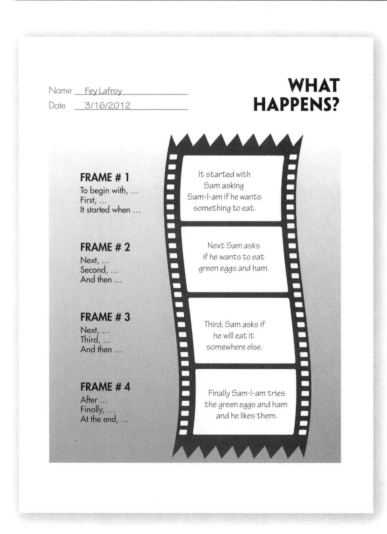

The students can decide the topic, or you may assign one. Instruct the students to write about the first event in the first frame, the second event in the second frame, the third event in the third frame, and the conclusion in the final, fourth frame.

Encourage the students to accompany their event statements with a visual or picture. For younger students, pictures and visuals can be used in place of written statements.

Name _____

Date _____

WHAT HAPPENS?

FRAME # 1

To begin with, …
First, …
It started when …

FRAME # 2

Next, …
Second, …
And then …

FRAME # 3

Next, …
Third, …
And then …

FRAME # 4

After …
Finally, …
At the end, …

65 Time Line

Medium

Easy   Hard

► Grades: K–5
► Level of Difficulty: Medium-Hard

Overview

Another sequencing graphic organizer, the Time Line supports students to organize events into chronological order.

Tips for Classroom Implementation

Instruct the students to select the important events in a narrative text or historical event. Put the date in the date blanks and then write what happened in the corresponding space. Encourage the students to add visuals; they can also use different colored markers and pencils for each event. This helps students to organize the information.

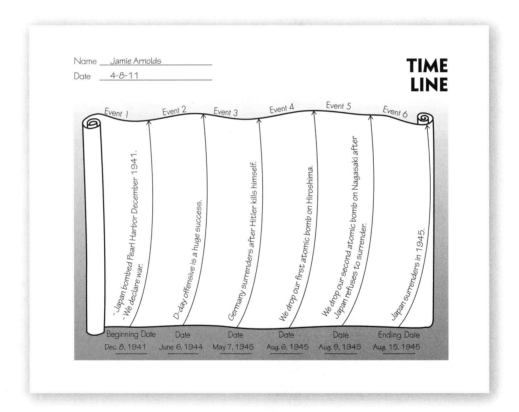

TIME LINE

Name _____

Date _____

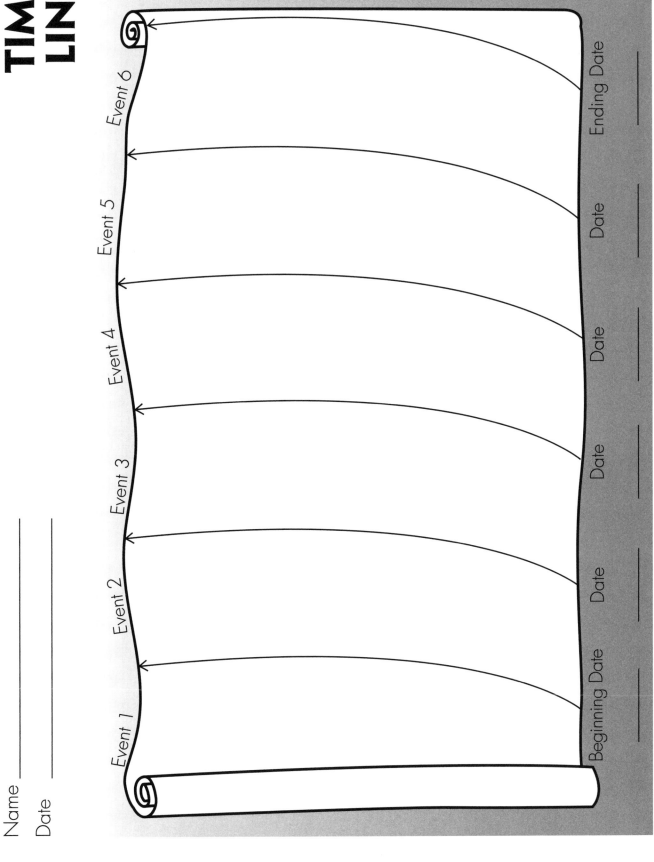

Event 1

Event 2

Event 3

Event 4

Event 5

Event 6

Beginning Date _____

Date _____

Date _____

Date _____

Date _____

Ending Date _____

66 Five Ws Chart

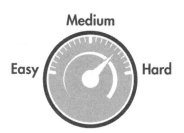

▶ Grades: K–5
▶ Level of Difficulty: Medium-Hard

Overview

Journalists answer the five Ws: Who, What, Where, When, and Why. These questions enable journalists to develop complete and informative stories. These questions are also essential for student writing and reading. As students answer these questions, they develop better comprehension and ability to articulate what they know and understand in their own writing.

Tips for Classroom Implementation

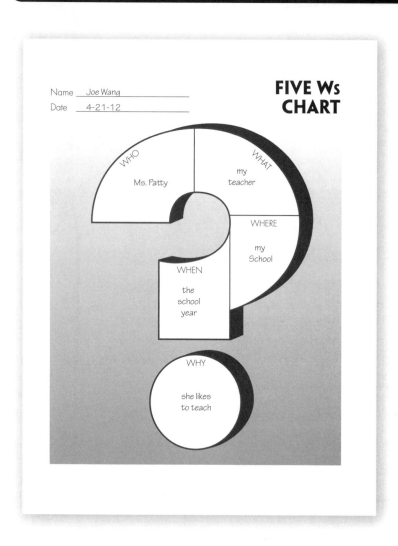

You will need to model this graphic organizer. After they have filled out the organizer, asking students the additional questions "What do you know now?" and "Why is it important?" fosters personal response and greater comprehension. I love to ask my students these questions. I learn a great deal about their thinking and what I need to do next as their teacher. It is through reflection, as prompted by these questions, that students are more likely to synthesize what they are learning.

Name _____

Date _____

FIVE Ws CHART

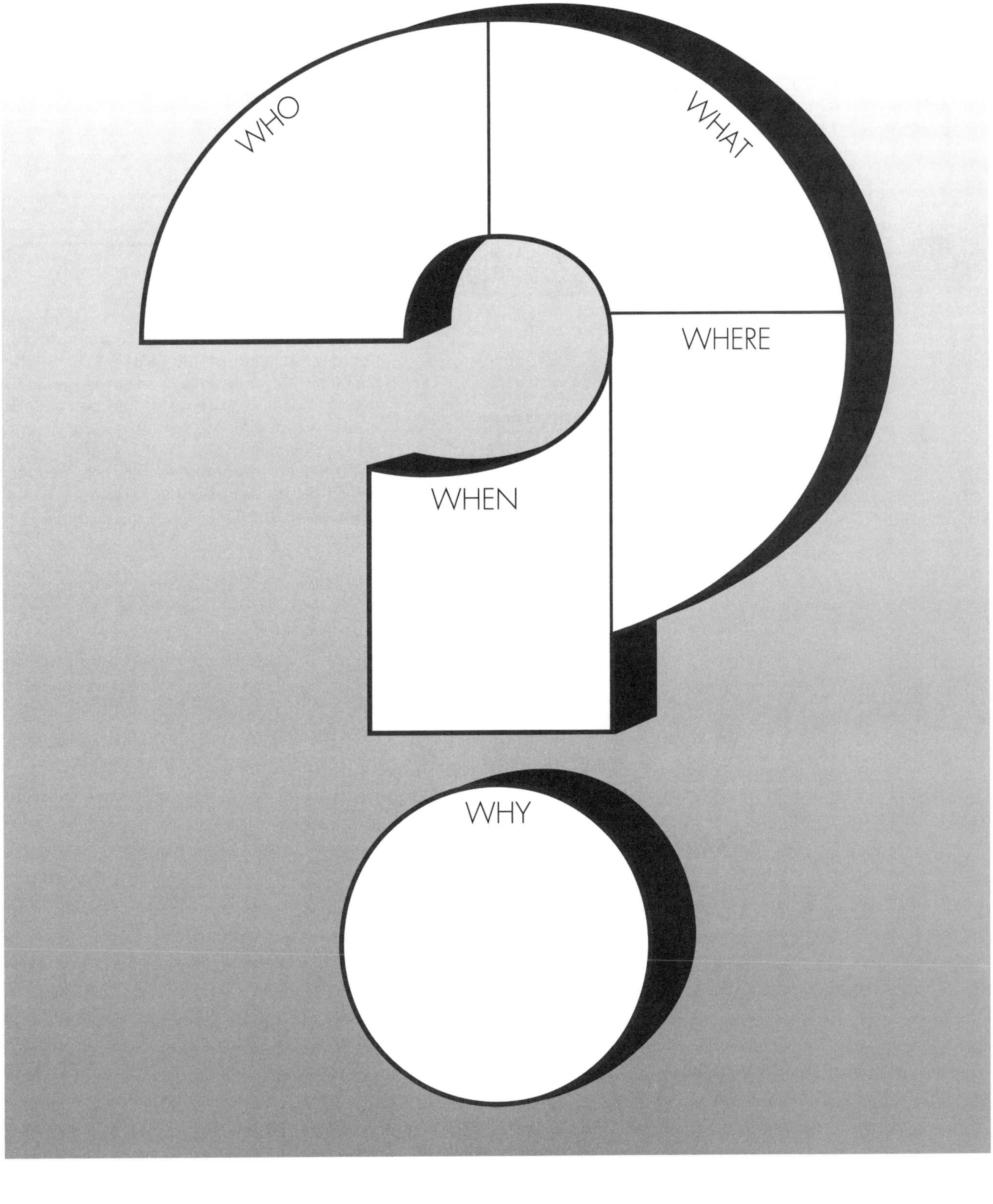

WHO

WHAT

WHERE

WHEN

WHY

Copyright © 2013 by John Wiley & Sons, Inc.

Graphic Organizers for Literacy 145

67 Observation Chart

► Grades: 3–5
► Level of Difficulty: Medium

Overview

This graphic organizer is useful for science subjects like biology, physical science, or chemistry. Students need to develop powers of observation to understand the nature of science. As the students record their observations, they are able to develop and test a hypothesis.

Tips for Classroom Implementation

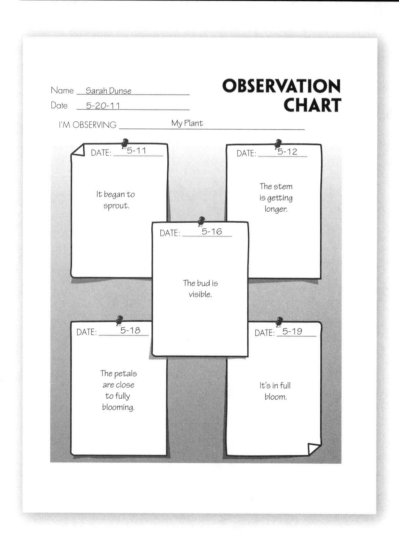

Instruct the students to think and brainstorm about what scientists do. Make a list of the characteristics and skills of scientists, remembering that one of these should be that scientists are good observers. Through a large group discussion, discuss the characteristics and elements of good observers: they need to record details, be attentive, and guess what might happen.

Name _____

Date _____

OBSERVATION CHART

I'M OBSERVING _____

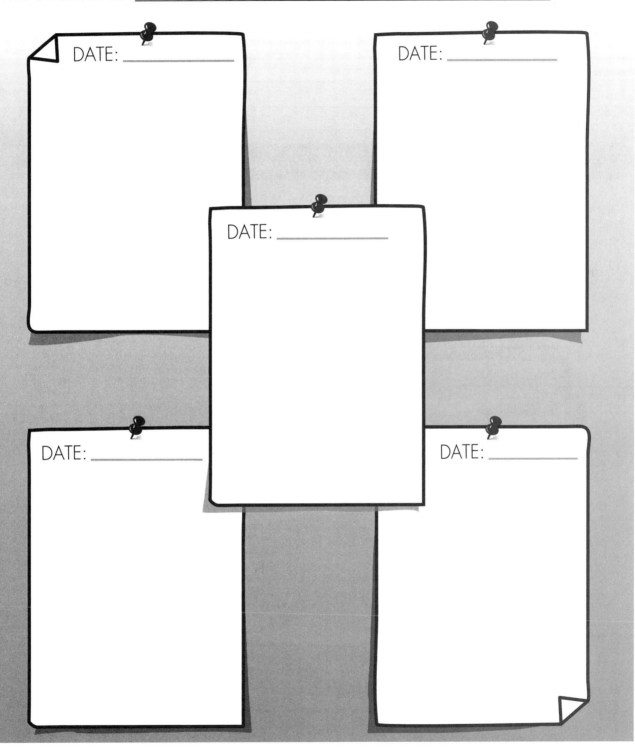

DATE: _____

DATE: _____

DATE: _____

DATE: _____

DATE: _____

68 Inverted Topic Triangle

► Grades: 2–5
► Level of Difficulty: Medium

Overview

It's challenging for most students to decide on a research topic that is specific and narrow in focus. This graphic organizer provides a structure for each student to explore a topic and then narrow it down for manageable research and writing.

Tips for Classroom Implementation

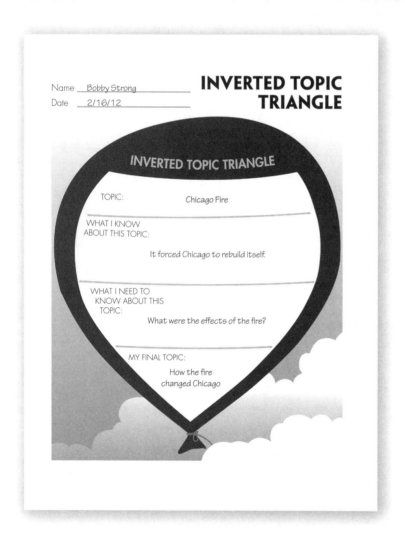

Model this graphic organizer in a Think Aloud through large group instruction. Take a subject familiar to the students and write that at the top of the triangle. Continue to narrow it down until you reach the bottom of the chart. Different color markers for each section can facilitate the students' understanding and organization of the topic.

Name _____

Date _____

INVERTED TOPIC TRIANGLE

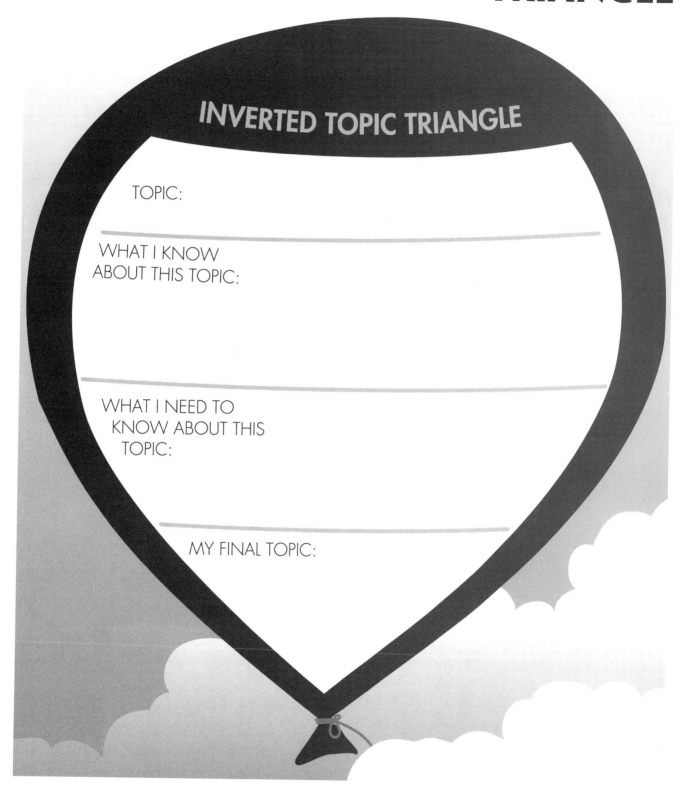

INVERTED TOPIC TRIANGLE

TOPIC:

WHAT I KNOW
ABOUT THIS TOPIC:

WHAT I NEED TO
KNOW ABOUT THIS
TOPIC:

MY FINAL TOPIC:

69 Literature Circle Roles

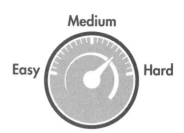

► Grades: 3–5
► Level of Difficulty: Medium-Hard

Overview

We all owe a debt of gratitude to teacher, author, and consultant Harvey "Smokey" Daniels. Thanks to him, literature circles are a well-known strategy for engaging learners. In a literature circle, students have roles that they must fill when discussing their assigned reading.

Tips for Classroom Implementation

If you are not already familiar with literature circles, I strongly suggest that you review the following resources to get started with literature circles:

H. Daniels & N. Steineke, *Mini-lessons for Literature Circles* (Portsmouth, NH: Heinemann, 2004).

The following webinar is available from the National Council of Teachers of English:

Literature Circles: Focusing on Differentiated Instruction https://secure.ncte.org/store/on-demand-literature-circles

LITERATURE CIRCLE ROLES

Discussion Director

"Captain" of the literature circle. The Discussion Director creates questions to help everyone understand the text. The Discussion Director asks questions like "who, what, why, when, where, how, and what if."

Vocabulary Detective

Finds words that the group may not know.

Helps the circle to learn about the words that they may not know.

Illustrator

Draws pictures and creates visualizations of important scenes or characters.

Checker

Makes sure that everyone participates and completes the literature circle tasks.

70   Journaling

▶ Grades: 3–5
▶ Level of Difficulty: Medium–Hard

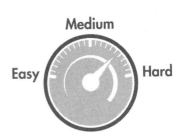

Overview

Journaling is an important practice for students to develop writing skills and fluency of ideas. There is substantial research supporting the role of journaling in the development of student writing skills. It is also an important activity for students to learn and understand new content.

   **Tips for Classroom Implementation**

It is important to model journaling with students so that they understand the expectations. Your modeling can help them make the most of this opportunity to explore and understand ideas through writing.

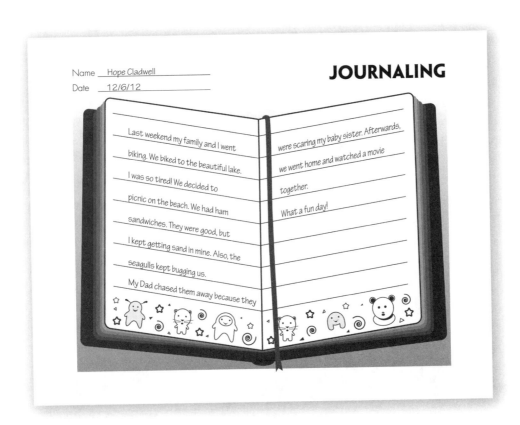

JOURNALING

Name _____

Date _____

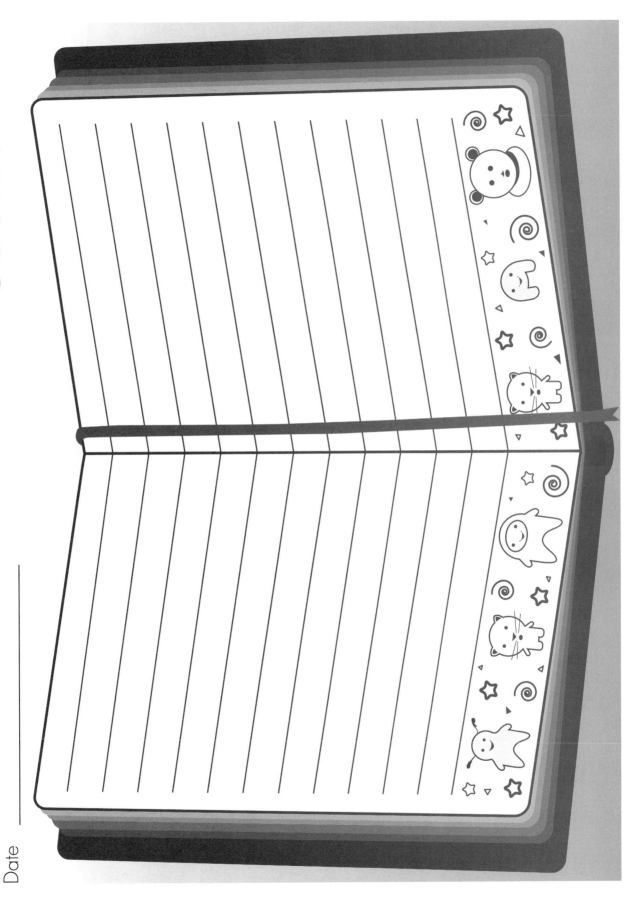

71 Entrance Slip

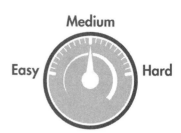

▶ Grades: 2–5
▶ Level of Difficulty: Medium

Overview

This graphic organizer prompts students to draw from their prior knowledge and serves as an introduction to a new unit or topic. Entrance Slips are one of the most frequently used content literacy strategies because they are so adaptable. The Entrance Slip strategy is an effective tool for previewing content at the beginning of a lesson. This activity facilitates students' focusing on the topic of the lesson and what they will be learning.

Tips for Classroom Implementation

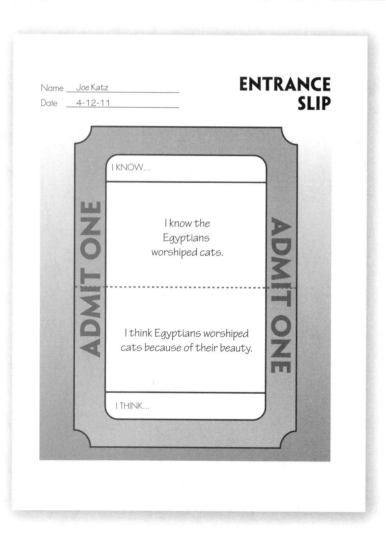

You may want to model the Entrance Slip for the students. Distribute the Entrance Slip at the beginning of a lesson and give students three minutes to record their responses.

Name _____

Date _____

ENTRANCE SLIP

ADMIT ONE

ADMIT ONE

I KNOW...

I THINK...

72 Exit Slip

▶ Grades: 2–5
▶ Level of Difficulty: Easy-Medium-Hard

Overview

This graphic organizer prompts students to think about what they have learned. When students immediately take time to think about their learning, it is much more likely to become part of their long-term memory and personal knowledge. Exit Slips are one of the most commonly used content literacy strategies and also an effective means of assessment. Many teachers use Exit Slips to determine how well students understand content. Exit Slips also make students accountable for what they have learned.

Tips for Classroom Implementation

Use the Exit Slip as a closure activity. Distribute the Exit Slips and instruct students to think about what they have learned and why it is important.

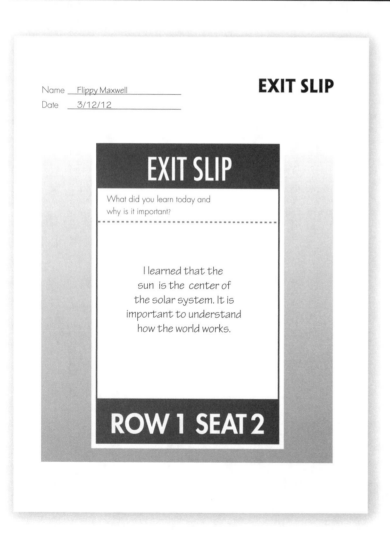

Name _____

Date _____

EXIT SLIP

What did you learn today and
why is it important?

- -

ROW 1 SEAT 2

73 Character Description

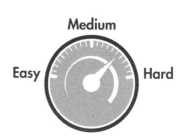

▶ Grades: K–5
▶ Level of Difficulty: Medium-Hard

Overview

Students can use this graphic organizer to develop a character to use in a narrative story. It can also be used to analyze a character from a story.

Tips for Classroom Implementation

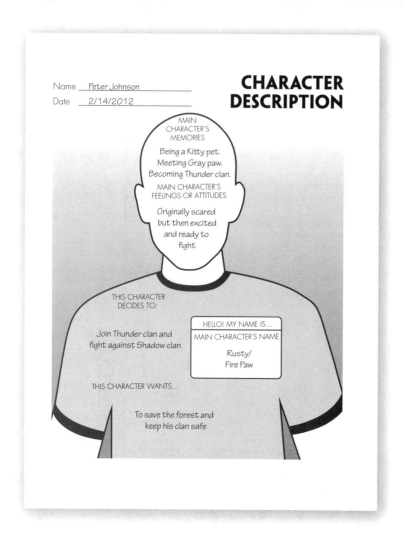

Name __Peter Johnson__
Date __2/14/2012__

CHARACTER DESCRIPTION

MAIN CHARACTER'S MEMORIES

Being a Kitty pet.
Meeting Gray paw.
Becoming Thunder clan.

MAIN CHARACTER'S FEELINGS OR ATTITUDES

Originally scared but then excited and ready to fight

THIS CHARACTER DECIDES TO:

Join Thunder clan and fight against Shadow clan

HELLO! MY NAME IS…
MAIN CHARACTER'S NAME

Rusty/
Fire Paw

THIS CHARACTER WANTS…

To save the forest and keep his clan safe

Model how to use this graphic organizer, perhaps using a character with whom the students are familiar. The students can work in pairs or as individuals as they complete this graphic organizer/character analysis. Students also enjoy sharing their characters with each other.

Name _____

Date _____

CHARACTER DESCRIPTION

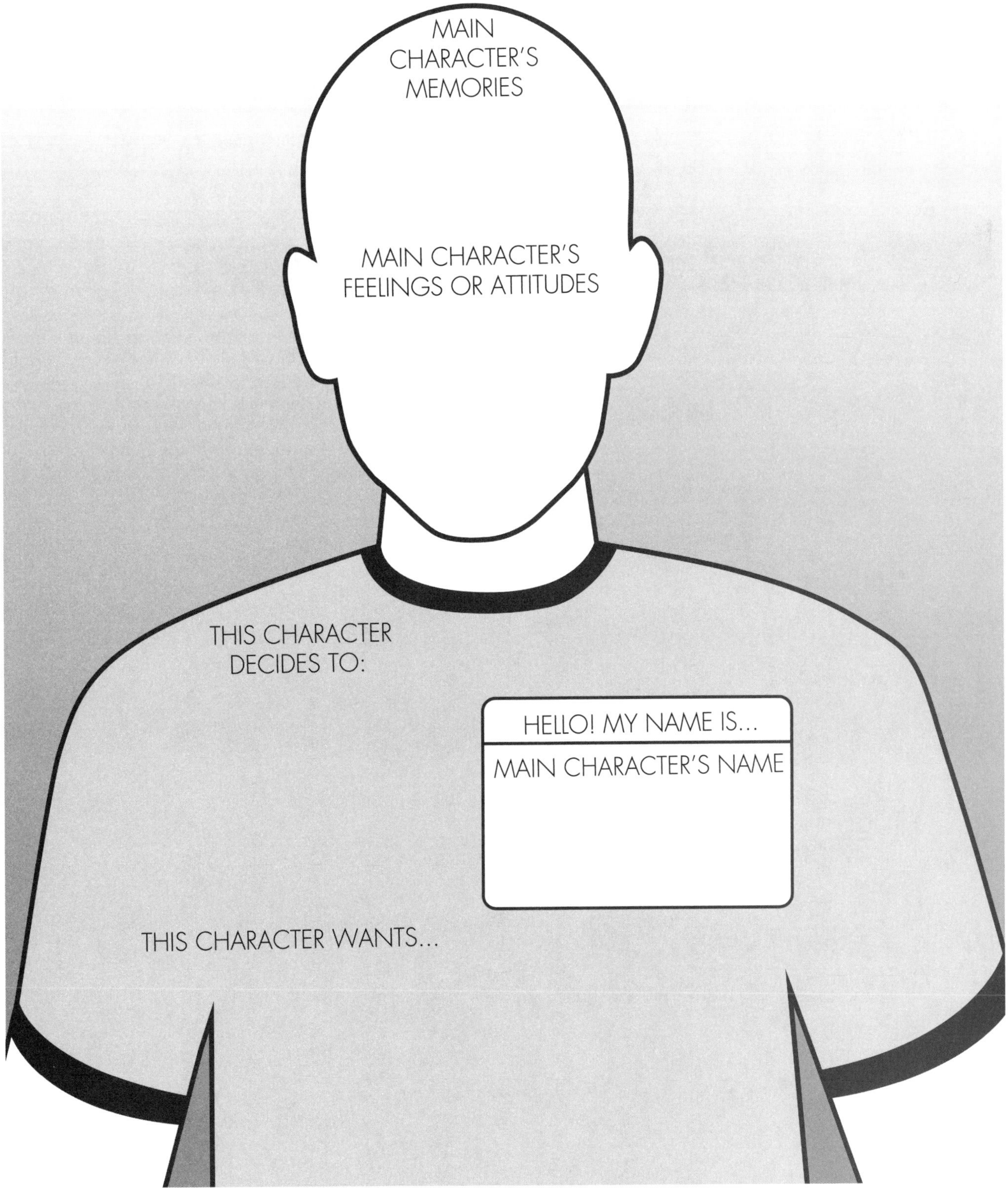

MAIN
CHARACTER'S
MEMORIES

MAIN CHARACTER'S
FEELINGS OR ATTITUDES

THIS CHARACTER
DECIDES TO:

HELLO! MY NAME IS...

MAIN CHARACTER'S NAME

THIS CHARACTER WANTS...

74 Adding Details

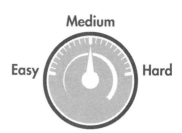
Medium
Easy — Hard

▶ Grades: 2–5
▶ Level of Difficulty: Medium

Overview

Details help us to understand new content. This graphic organizer encourages students to add information and details from many sources in order to fully understand new content.

Tips for Classroom Implementation

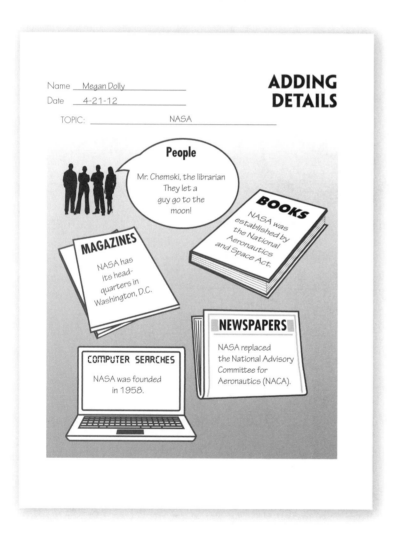

Brainstorm with the students about sources from which we gain new information: people, books, newspapers, and so on. Discuss how each of these sources can help us to understand and learn about new content. I like to have the students work in pairs or groups of three when they use this graphic organizer.

Name _____

Date _____

TOPIC: _____

75 Who, What, Where, When, Why, How

▶ Grades: 2–5
▶ Level of Difficulty: Medium-Hard

Medium

Easy   **Hard**

Overview

Effective learners, writers, and thinkers ask Who, What, Where, When and Why. This graphic organizer pushes students to more deeply consider information by adding "how". This prompts students to reflect and articulate what they learned. These questions are essential for writing and reading text and for students to become effective writers, readers, and learners. As students answer these questions, they develop better comprehension and ability to articulate what they know and understand.

Tips for Classroom Implementation

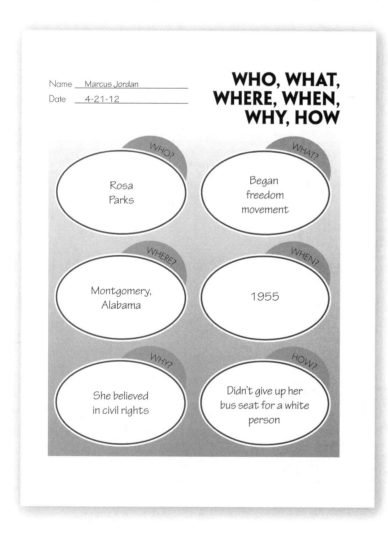

You will need to model this graphic organizer. After they have filled out the organizer, asking students the additional questions "What do you know now?" and "Why is it important?" fosters personal response and greater comprehension. I love to ask my students these questions. I learn a great deal about their thinking and what I need to do next as their teacher. It is through reflection, as prompted by these questions, that students are more likely to synthesize what they are learning. The final question "How?" prompts students to predict and extend their learning even further.

Name _____

Date _____

WHO, WHAT, WHERE, WHEN, WHY, HOW

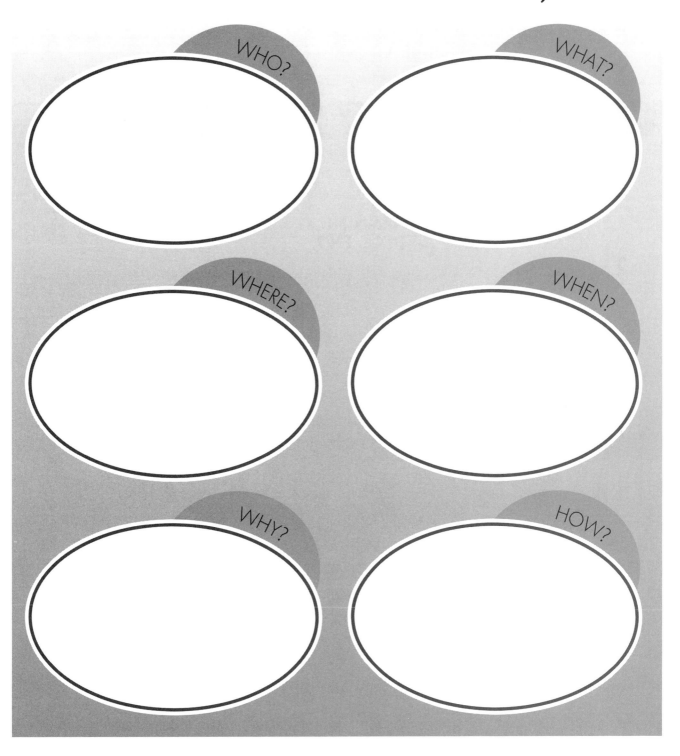

WHO?

WHAT?

WHERE?

WHEN?

WHY?

HOW?

76 Beginning, Middle, End

► Grades: K–5
► Level of Difficulty: Medium-Hard

Overview

This graphic organizer helps students organize story ideas and details into the fundamental story sequence of beginning, middle, and end.

Tips for Classroom Implementation

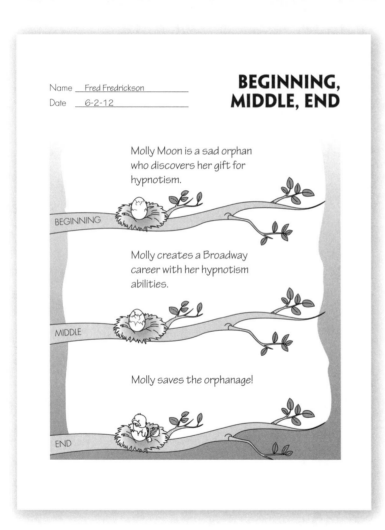

Name _Fred Fredrickson_
Date _6-2-12_

BEGINNING, MIDDLE, END

BEGINNING
Molly Moon is a sad orphan who discovers her gift for hypnotism.

MIDDLE
Molly creates a Broadway career with her hypnotism abilities.

END
Molly saves the orphanage!

You may want to use a story with which the students are already familiar to model this graphic organizer. Have the students use the organizer as a prewriting activity. This allows them to sketch the basic outline of the story.

Name _____

Date _____

BEGINNING, MIDDLE, END

BEGINNING

MIDDLE

END

77 Situation, Problem, Solution

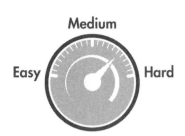

▶ Grades: 2–5
▶ Level of Difficulty: Medium-Hard

Overview

Similar to the Beginning, Middle, End graphic organizer, teaching basic narrative writing and problem solving with this graphic organizer helps students to focus and identify key information.

Tips for Classroom Implementation

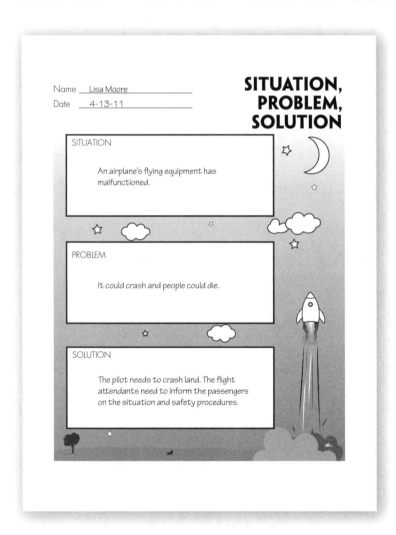

You may want to pose a problem that is of high interest for the students; for example, "There is a lot of pollution in our world" or "There are endangered animals."

Write the problem that you are modeling in the corresponding space on the graphic organizer. Continue to model questions and solutions to solve the problem using the graphic organizer. I like to use this graphic organizer for homework or as an assessment. As students are studying a unit, they can identify problems and predict possible solutions through the questions that they pose.

Name _____

Date _____

SITUATION, PROBLEM, SOLUTION

SITUATION

PROBLEM

SOLUTION

78 Autobiography Organizer

▶ Grades: 2–5
▶ Level of Difficulty: Medium

Overview

This graphic organizer supports students' learning to organize details and information to write an autobiography.

Tips for Classroom Implementation

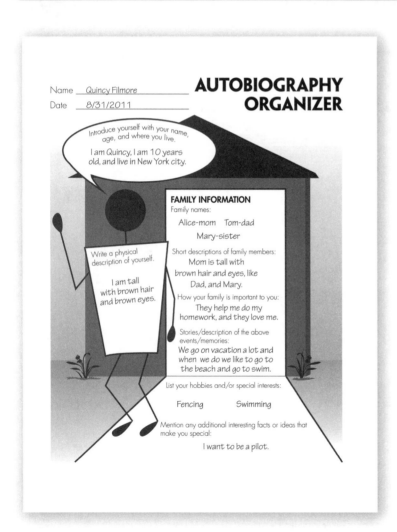

Model the graphic organizer with information about yourself. Next, draft an autobiography that contains the information that you included on the graphic organizer.

Name _____

Date _____

AUTOBIOGRAPHY ORGANIZER

Introduce yourself with your name, age, and where you live.

Write a physical description of yourself.

FAMILY INFORMATION

Family names:

Short descriptions of family members:

How your family is important to you:

Stories/description of the above events/memories:

List your hobbies and/or special interests:

Mention any additional interesting facts or ideas that make you special:

79 Story Builder for Writing

▶ Grades: K–5
▶ Level of Difficulty: Medium

Medium

Easy   Hard

Overview

All stories have common elements; problem, solution, characters, and setting. Using a graphic organizer to record ideas and plans for a story is a useful prewriting activity.

Tips for Classroom Implementation

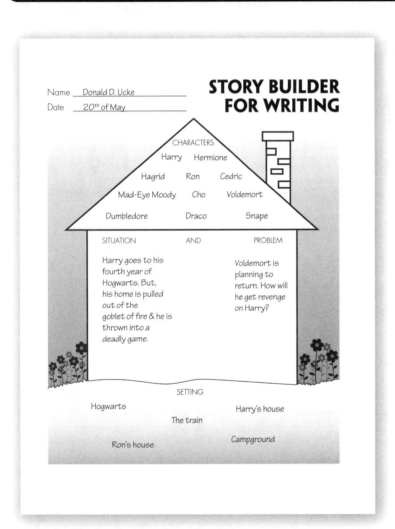

Name   Donald D. Ucke

Date   20ᵗʰ of May

STORY BUILDER FOR WRITING

CHARACTERS

Harry   Hermione

Hagrid   Ron   Cedric

Mad-Eye Moody   Cho   Voldemort

Dumbledore   Draco   Snape

SITUATION   AND   PROBLEM

Harry goes to his fourth year of Hogwarts. But, his home is pulled out of the goblet of fire & he is thrown into a deadly game.

Voldemort is planning to return. How will he get revenge on Harry?

SETTING

Hogwarts   Harry's house

The train

Ron's house   Campground

As you model this graphic organizer for the students, be sure to review story elements. Like house builders, writers use the story elements to create an interesting story.

Name _____

Date _____

STORY BUILDER
FOR WRITING

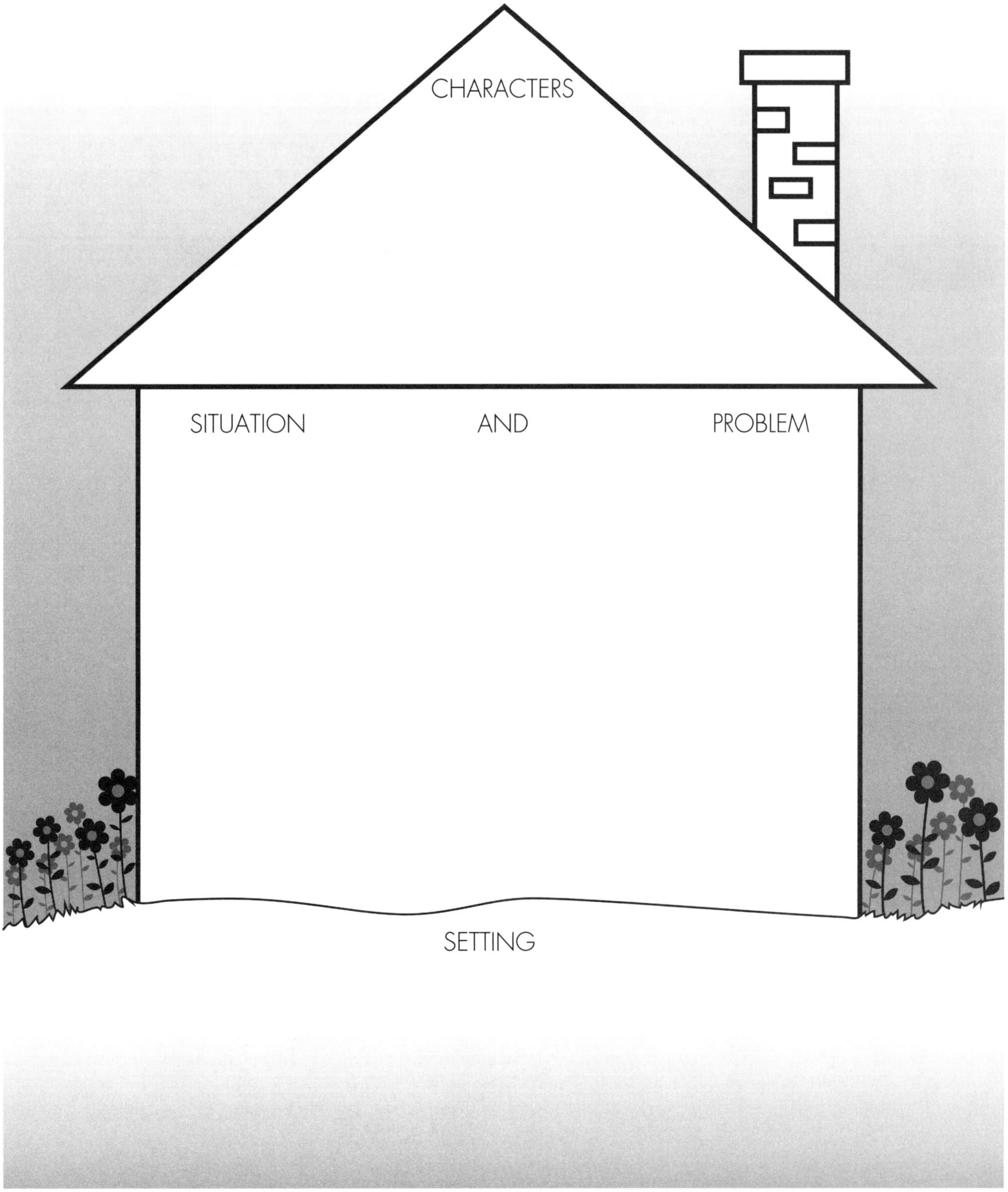

CHARACTERS

SITUATION   AND   PROBLEM

SETTING

80 Finding Resources

▶ Grades: 3–5
▶ Level of Difficulty: Medium-Hard

Medium

Easy   Hard

Overview

In today's Information Age there are all kinds of ways in which we can harvest information. The Internet offers limitless platforms to discover, research, and learn about different subjects and content.

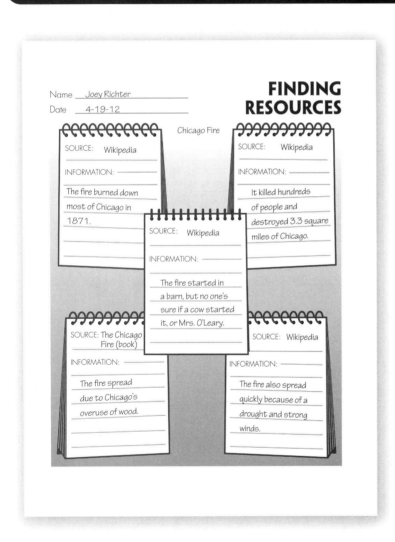

Tips for Classroom Implementation

Model for students how to use this graphic organizer to record different sources of information. Encourage the students to use a wide variety of sources as they record the information in the provided spaces.

Name _____

Date _____

FINDING RESOURCES

SOURCE: _____
_____

INFORMATION: _____
_____
_____
_____
_____

SOURCE: _____
_____

INFORMATION: _____
_____
_____
_____
_____

SOURCE: _____
_____

INFORMATION: _____
_____
_____
_____
_____
_____

SOURCE: _____
_____

INFORMATION: _____
_____
_____
_____
_____

SOURCE: _____
_____

INFORMATION: _____
_____
_____
_____
_____

81 Main Ideas and Supporting Ideas

Medium

Easy — Hard

▶ Grades: 2–5
▶ Level of Difficulty: Medium-Hard

Overview

Learning how to identify the main idea in a text is an important skill for all readers. When students are able to identify and articulate the key information in text (main idea and supporting ideas), this leads to greater understanding and comprehension.

Tips for Classroom Implementation

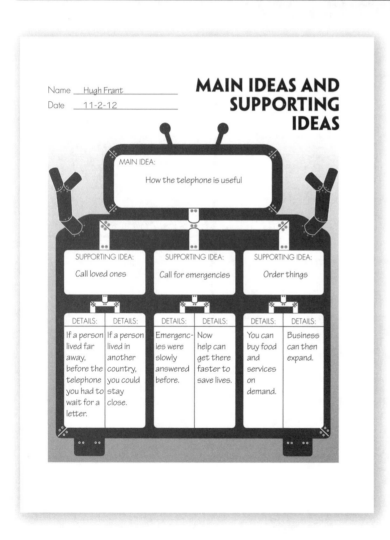

You will want to model this graphic organizer, and I strongly urge you to use different colored markers for each of the levels: main idea, supporting idea, and details.

As you model this graphic organizer through a Think Aloud, be sure to articulate to the students why and how you are selecting specific information as the main idea, supporting ideas, and details. I think that with this graphic organizer it is also helpful for the students to create visualizations for the corresponding information for each of the sections.

Name _____

Date _____

MAIN IDEAS AND SUPPORTING IDEAS

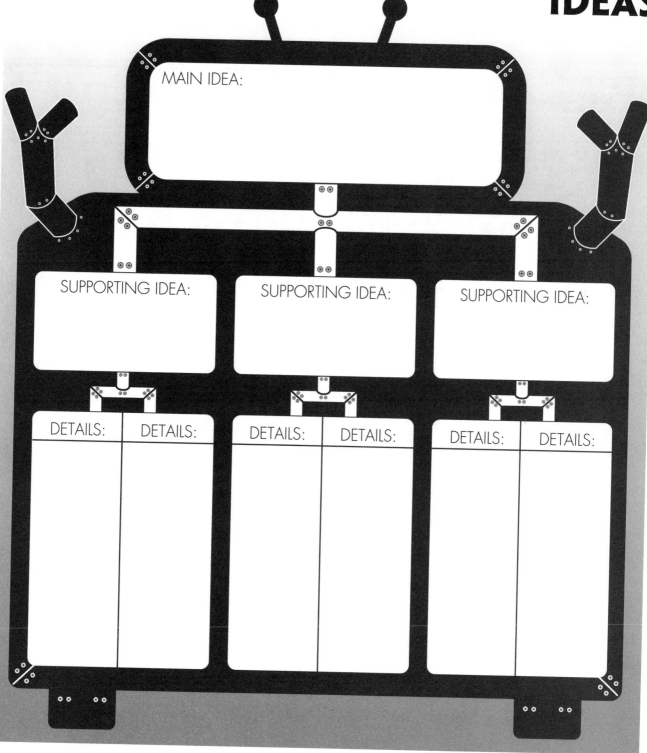

MAIN IDEA:

SUPPORTING IDEA:

SUPPORTING IDEA:

SUPPORTING IDEA:

DETAILS: | DETAILS:

DETAILS: | DETAILS:

DETAILS: | DETAILS:

Graphic Organizers 82 and 83: Book Reports

Overview

Students write many book reports in their school years. I have found that students are sometimes confused about what they should record and share through a book report. Graphic Organizers 82 and 83 offer a structure for students to write a book report for a nonfiction text and a fiction text.

Tips for Classroom Implementation

Share the book report graphic organizer that you plan to use with the students prior to their reading. In doing so, your expectations for the students' reports are clearly articulated. Students also learn when literacy models, like teachers, share how they read and think about texts. Model for these students your responses for these graphic organizers so that they can benefit from witnessing a literacy model in action.

When you share these graphic organizers with the students, model how to complete it through large group instruction or through a literacy center. Once the students learn how to use the format, you can have them work individually or in pairs. For younger students, the class could complete the graphic organizer as a large group after a Read Aloud. For older students, the graphic organizers may be used independently or even in literature circles or guided reading.

82 Nonfiction Book Report

▶ Grades: 2–5
▶ Level of Difficulty: Medium

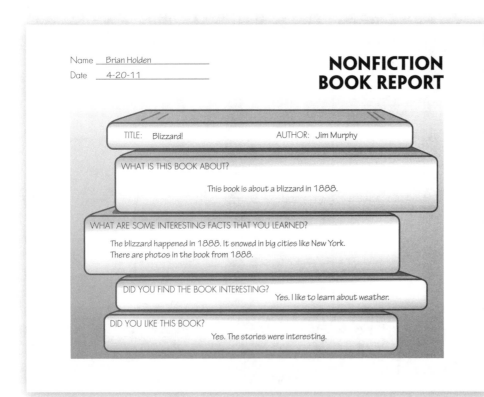

Name __Brian Holden__
Date __4-20-11__

NONFICTION BOOK REPORT

TITLE: Blizzard!   AUTHOR: Jim Murphy

WHAT IS THIS BOOK ABOUT?
This book is about a blizzard in 1888.

WHAT ARE SOME INTERESTING FACTS THAT YOU LEARNED?
The blizzard happened in 1888. It snowed in big cities like New York. There are photos in the book from 1888.

DID YOU FIND THE BOOK INTERESTING? Yes. I like to learn about weather.

DID YOU LIKE THIS BOOK?
Yes. The stories were interesting.

Name _____

Date _____

NONFICTION BOOK REPORT

TITLE:

AUTHOR:

WHAT IS THIS BOOK ABOUT?

WHAT ARE SOME INTERESTING FACTS THAT YOU LEARNED?

DID YOU FIND THE BOOK INTERESTING?

DID YOU LIKE THIS BOOK?

83 Fiction Book Report

▶ Grades: 2–5
▶ Level of Difficulty: Medium

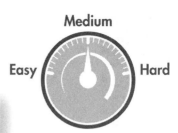

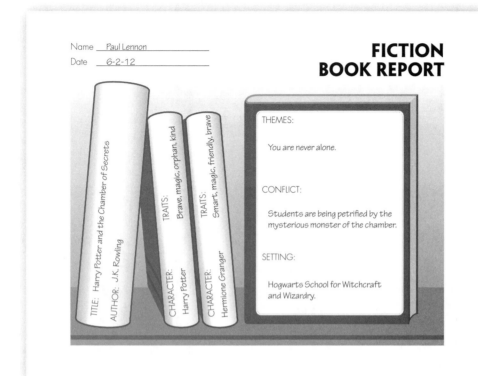

Name Paul Lennon
Date 6-2-12

FICTION BOOK REPORT

TITLE: Harry Potter and the Chamber of Secrets
AUTHOR: J.K. Rowling

TRAITS:
Brave, magic, orphan, kind

CHARACTER:
Harry Potter

TRAITS:
Smart, magic, friendly, brave

CHARACTER:
Hermione Granger

THEMES:

You are never alone.

CONFLICT:

Students are being petrified by the mysterious monster of the chamber.

SETTING:

Hogwarts School for Witchcraft and Wizardry.

FICTION
BOOK REPORT

Name _____

Date _____

THEMES:

CONFLICT:

SETTING:

CHARACTER:

TRAITS:

CHARACTER:

TRAITS:

AUTHOR:

TITLE:

Graphic Organizers 84–86: Story Structures

Overview

Part of the writing process for young writers is learning about a wide variety of genres. As students learn about different Story Structures, they are adding to their repertoire of formats that they might use for their own writing.

Tips for Classroom Implementation

When you share these graphic organizers with the students, model how to complete them through large group instruction or through a literacy center. Once the students learn how to use the format, you can have them work individually or in pairs to create stories based on the structures featured in these graphic organizers. For younger students, the class could complete the graphic organizer as a large group and even act it out. For older students, the graphic organizers may be used independently as a prewriting activity or to get them started in a writing workshop setting.

84 Newspaper Article

▶ Grades: 3–5
▶ Level of Difficulty: Medium

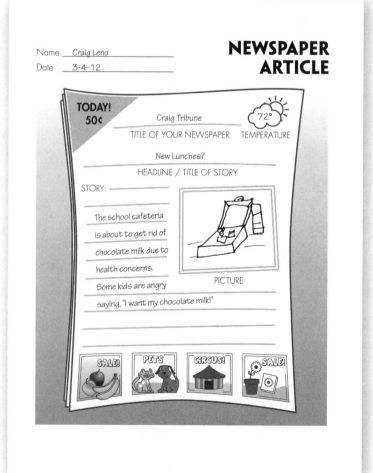

NEWSPAPER ARTICLE

TODAY!
50¢

TITLE OF YOUR NEWSPAPER

TEMPERATURE

HEADLINE / TITLE OF STORY

STORY: _____

_____

_____

_____

_____

PICTURE

_____

_____

_____

_____

SALE!

PETS

CIRCUS!

SALE!

85 Animal Story

▶ Grades: K–5
▶ Level of Difficulty: Medium

Medium
Easy   Hard

Overview

See the notes at the beginning of this section.

 Tips for Classroom Implementation

See the notes at the beginning of this section.

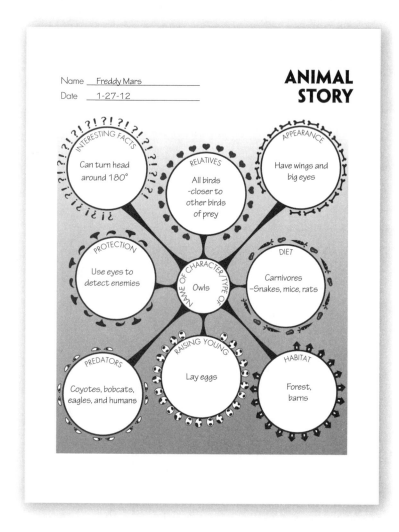

Name _____

Date _____

ANIMAL STORY

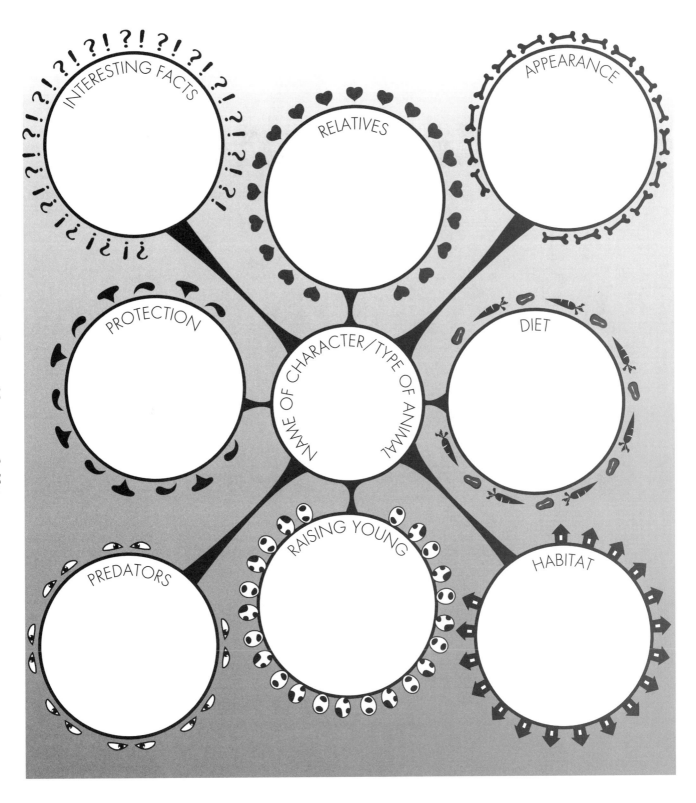

INTERESTING FACTS

RELATIVES

APPEARANCE

PROTECTION

NAME OF CHARACTER/TYPE OF ANIMAL

DIET

PREDATORS

RAISING YOUNG

HABITAT

86 Fairy Tale Story

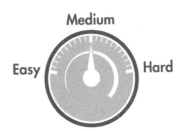

▶ Grades: K–5
▶ Level of Difficulty: Medium

Overview

See the notes at the beginning of this section.

 Tips for Classroom Implementation

See the notes at the beginning of this section.

Name _____

Date _____

FAIRY TALE STORY

GOOD CHARACTER:

BAD CHARACTER:

MAGIC:

STORY:

HAPPY ENDING:

CHAPTER SIX
Graphic Organizers for Specific Subjects: Social Studies, Science, and Mathematics

87 Coat of Arms

▶ Grades: 2–5
▶ Level of Difficulty: Medium

Overview

Social studies, especially history, provides students with the opportunity to discover how places, people, times, and events comprise major events. This graphic organizer helps students to collect, record, analyze, and represent important information that facilitates comprehension of major historical events.

Tips for Classroom Implementation

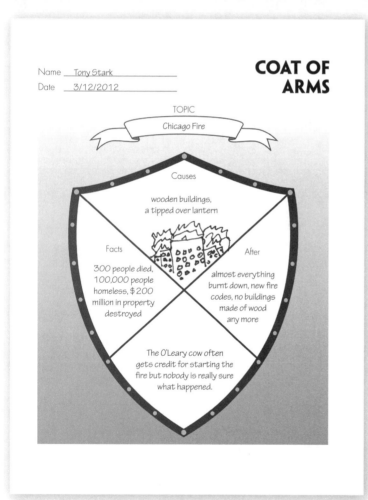

Name Tony Stark
Date 3/12/2012

COAT OF ARMS

TOPIC
Chicago Fire

Causes
wooden buildings,
a tipped over lantern

Facts
300 people died,
100,000 people
homeless, $200
million in property
destroyed

After
almost everything
burnt down, new fire
codes, no buildings
made of wood
any more

The O'Leary cow often
gets credit for starting the
fire but nobody is really sure
what happened.

Students should select a major event, topic, or key figure. Each quadrant of this graphic organizer can be labeled with subtopics. As students gather information, they can record key facts and details in the corresponding quadrant. Younger students can draw pictures and add key words. I strongly recommend that all students, no matter the age level, add visuals and pictures as a means to deepen understanding.

Name _____

Date _____

TOPIC

88 Flow Chart/Sequencing Events

▶ Grades: K–5
▶ Level of Difficulty: Medium-Hard

Overview

Sequencing events and information is an important skill for students to develop, as it leads to greater comprehension of new information and is also an important reading skill. The Flow Chart/Sequencing Events graphic organizer prompts students to identify key events and place them in a logical order.

Tips for Classroom Implementation

When I teach students about identifying key events sequencing, I generally instruct them to identify the first and last major event. Then I ask them to identify the events after the first major event that led to the final major events. Color coding, pictures, and visualizations are always useful for students to better identify and sequence events as they consider how the information is related.

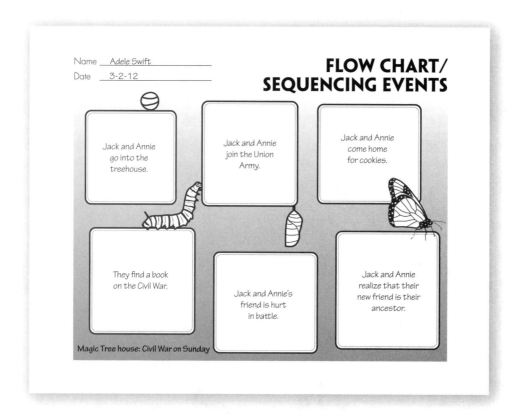

Name _Adele Swift_
Date _3-2-12_

FLOW CHART/ SEQUENCING EVENTS

Jack and Annie go into the treehouse.

Jack and Annie join the Union Army.

Jack and Annie come home for cookies.

They find a book on the Civil War.

Jack and Annie's friend is hurt in battle.

Jack and Annie realize that their new friend is their ancestor.

Magic Tree house: Civil War on Sunday

FLOW CHART/
SEQUENCING EVENTS

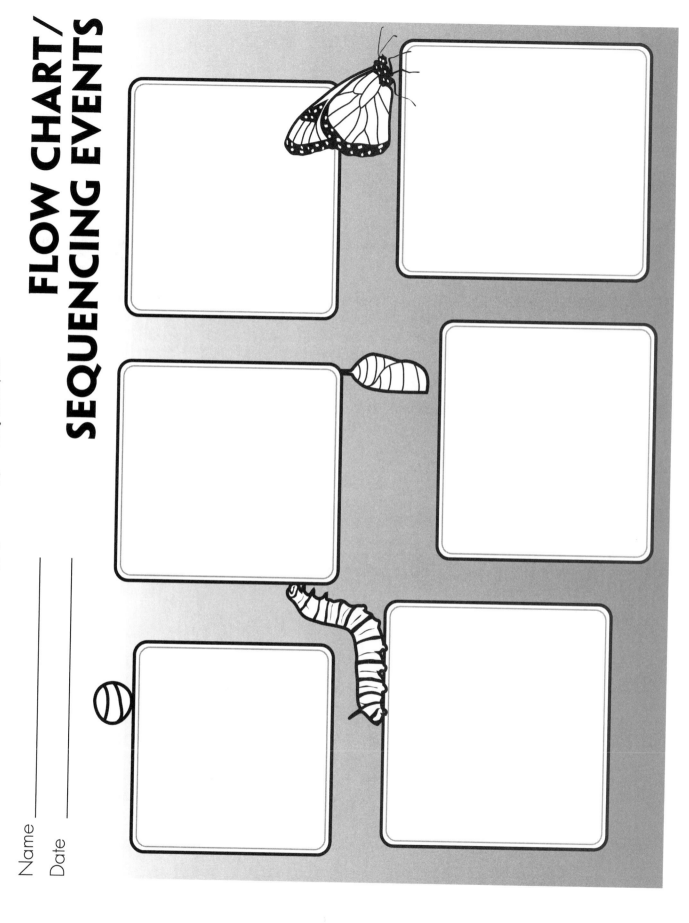

Name _____

Date _____

Graphic Organizers for Specific Subjects: Social Studies, Science, and Mathematics

89 History Trails

▶ Grades: K–5
▶ Level of Difficulty: Medium

Overview

Students will develop the following reading strategies:

- Connecting
- Using prior knowledge
- Predicting
- Visualizing
- Making inferences

This graphic organizer offers a structure for students to use to put the stages of an historical event into chronological order. An understanding of the key events facilitates greater exploration into the structure of the historical event.

Are the events related by cause and effect, do they connect as situation-problem-solution, or is the story simply one of beginning-middle-end? Recording the text and visual images of the key events also enhances students' comprehension.

Tips for Classroom Implementation

When you first introduce students to History Trails, select the key events through a large group discussion. As the students recall the events, arrange them in chronological order and instruct the students to reexamine these events for specific details that can be illustrated.

Name _____

Date _____

HISTORY TRAILS

Write down and illustrate the key events in chronological order.

90 Cause & Effect in History

▶ Grades: 2–5
▶ Level of Difficulty: Medium-Hard

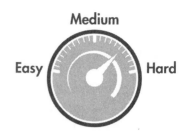

Overview

Understanding causal relationships is a skill that, in turn, develops student critical-thinking skills. When students are able to identify causes and effects, they are better able to understand causal relationships.

Tips for Classroom Implementation

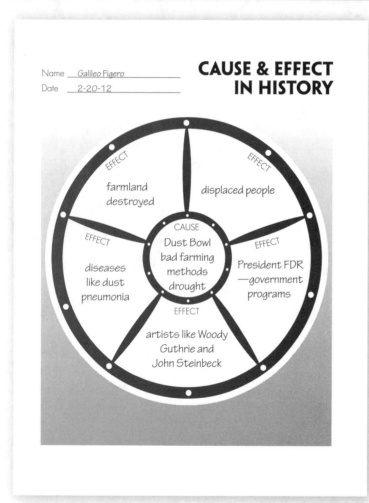

Name *Galileo Figero*
Date *2-20-12*

CAUSE & EFFECT IN HISTORY

EFFECT — farmland destroyed

EFFECT — displaced people

CAUSE — Dust Bowl bad farming methods drought

EFFECT — diseases like dust pneumonia

EFFECT — President FDR —government programs

EFFECT — artists like Woody Guthrie and John Steinbeck

When you introduce this graphic organizer, make sure that you review the fact that a cause makes an effect occur. You may want to provide some examples of causes and effects and model how to complete this graphic organizer.

Name _____

Date _____

CAUSE & EFFECT
IN HISTORY

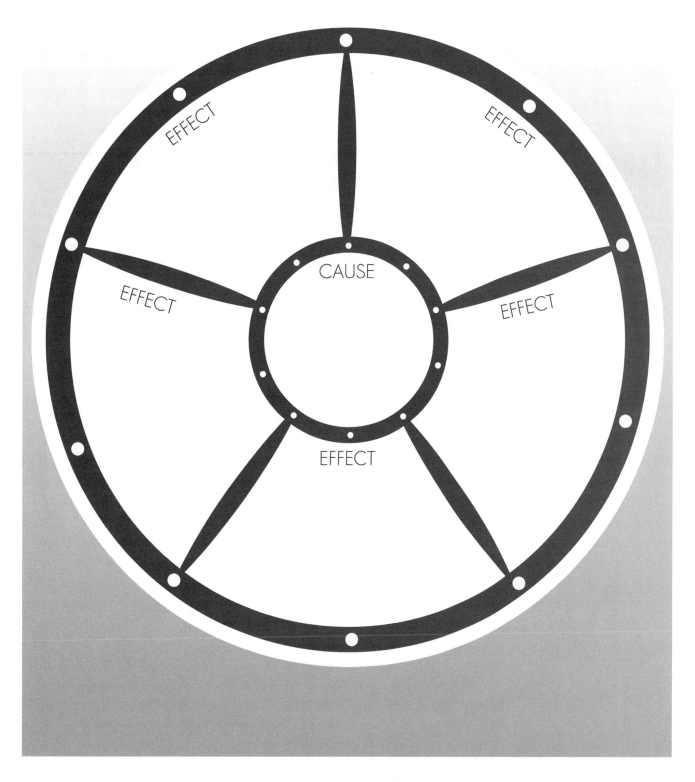

91 Mapping It Out

▶ Grades: 1–5
▶ Level of Difficulty: Medium

Overview

Visualizing geographical information supports students in developing an understanding of spatial forms and relationships. As students think about visualizing geographical features, they develop a greater sense of the location by placing themselves there.

Tips for Classroom Implementation

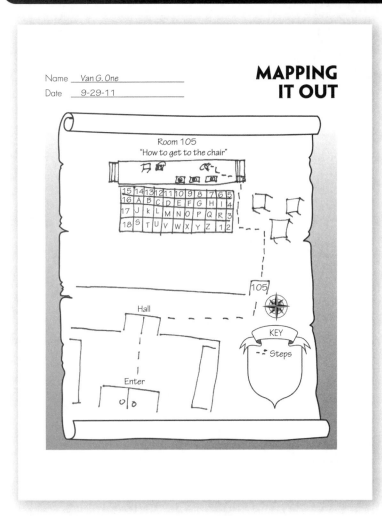

Name Van G. One

Date 9-29-11

MAPPING IT OUT

Model this graphic organizer for the students by choosing an object in the classroom. Point out the details of the object and how to represent them on the map. Encourage the students to include details like numbers, colors, or symbols to create a map key.

Name _____

Date _____

MAPPING IT OUT

KEY

92   Sort and Classify

▶ Grades: 2–5
▶ Level of Difficulty: Medium

Overview

Being able to sort and classify information is an important skill for students to develop, as it in turn supports critical-thinking skills. When students make decisions about sorting and categorizing, they are making decisions about how information is grouped and related.

Tips for Classroom Implementation

Model for the students how to complete this graphic organizer with actual physical objects, if possible. As you model your sorting and classifying, be sure to narrate your thinking for the students.

Name _____

Date _____

SORT THE OBJECTS INTO THE DIFFERENT BUCKETS.
NAME EACH GROUP.

GROUP:

GROUP:

GROUP:

93 Observation Diary

▶ Grades: 2–5
▶ Level of Difficulty: Medium-Hard

Overview

Learning how to pay attention to details and events is a critical skill for scientists. This graphic organizer provides a structure students can use to record and share observation.

Tips for Classroom Implementation

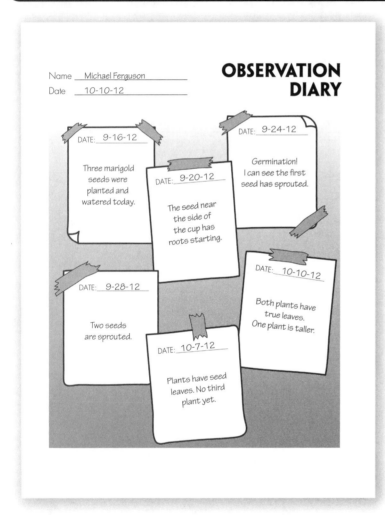

Brainstorm with the students about what scientists do and what they want to accomplish. Explain to the students that scientists must be keen observers and record key details in order to answer questions and explain phenomena. You may want to have students work in groups or pairs.

Name _____

Date _____

OBSERVATION DIARY

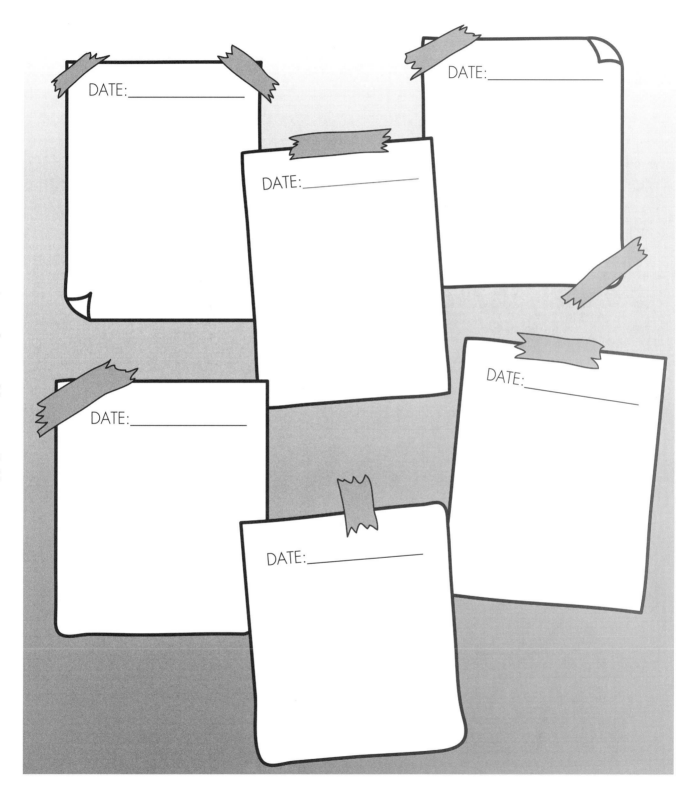

DATE:_____

DATE:_____

DATE:_____

DATE:_____

DATE:_____

DATE:_____

94 Inquiry Frame

▶ Grades: 1–4
▶ Level of Difficulty: Medium-Hard

Overview

Students will develop the following skills:

- Previewing
- Setting a purpose
- Connecting
- Using prior knowledge
- Predicting
- Visualizing
- Monitoring
- Making inferences

This graphic organizer prompts students to develop questions for exploration and discovery.

The concentric bands facilitate the connections between previous and newly acquired information in order to pose new questions.

Tips for Classroom Implementation

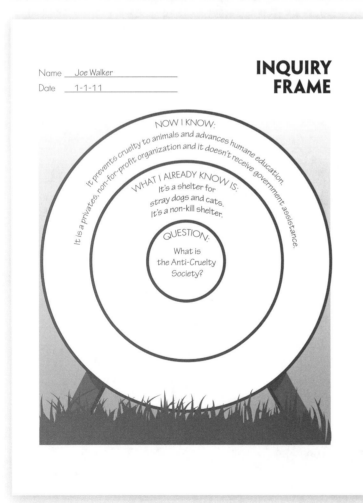

After filling out the Inquiry Frames organizer, the students can share their questions and develop a plan to answer those questions.

Name _____

Date _____

INQUIRY FRAME

NOW I KNOW:

WHAT I ALREADY KNOW IS:

QUESTION:

95 Science Fair Organizer

▶ Grades: 3–5
▶ Level of Difficulty: Medium

Medium

Easy   Hard

Overview

Science fairs are common events in elementary schools. One of the most challenging aspects of the science fair is identifying a topic. This graphic organizer will help students consider and narrow their focus to select a topic.

Tips for Classroom Implementation

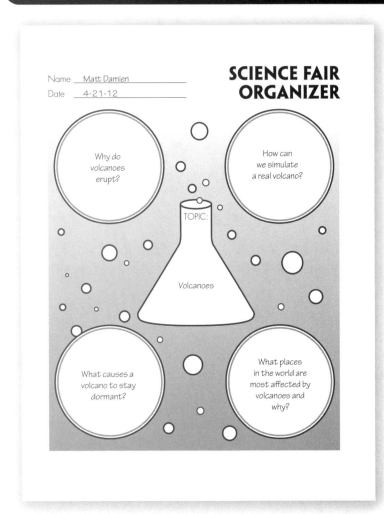

Through large group discussion, have the students brainstorm science fair projects. Pick a topic and model how to narrow it to a feasible science fair project.

Name _____

Date _____

SCIENCE FAIR ORGANIZER

TOPIC:

96 Inventor

▶ Grades: 3–5
▶ Level of Difficulty: Medium-Hard

Overview

The Inventor is a graphic organizer that supports students in developing an original idea, just like an inventor, to create something new.

Tips for Classroom Implementation

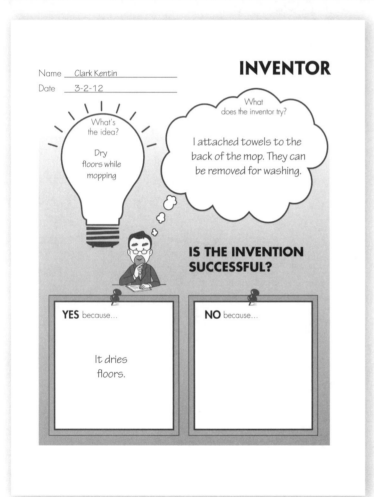

In a large group discussion, you may want to model this graphic organizer through a Think Aloud. Choose an invention with which the students are already quite familiar. Using the selected invention, take the students through the graphic organizer to model the process the inventor undertook to create something new.

INVENTOR

Name _____

Date _____

What's
the idea?

What
does the inventor try?

IS THE INVENTION SUCCESSFUL?

YES because…

NO because…

97 Scientific Method

▶ Grades: 2–5
▶ Level of Difficulty: Medium-Hard

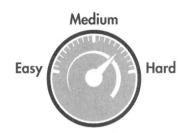

Overview

The Scientific Method graphic organizer outlines the five steps of the scientific method and provides a structure students can use to explore scientific questions and present experiment results.

Tips for Classroom Implementation

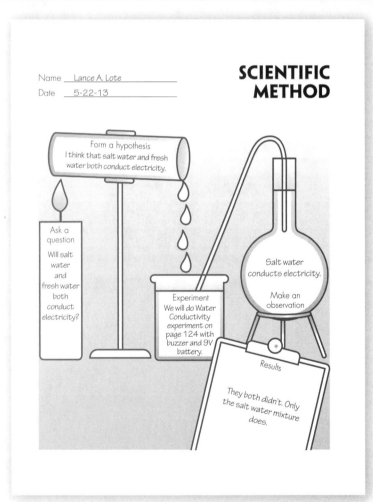

Name _Lance A. Lote_
Date _5-22-13_

SCIENTIFIC METHOD

Form a hypothesis
I think that salt water and fresh water both conduct electricity.

Ask a question
Will salt water and fresh water both conduct electricity?

Experiment
We will do Water Conductivity experiment on page 124 with buzzer and 9V battery.

Salt water conducts electricity.

Make an observation

Results
They both didn't. Only the salt water mixture does.

Review with students the steps of the scientific method and explain how scientists use it to create consistency in scientific inquiry. To model the scientific process, have the students pose a question to explore and answer. Guide the students to create a prediction based on the question. Remind the students that the prediction is a hypothesis. Model for the students how to explore, record the information, and be able to interpret the data the students collected.

SCIENTIFIC METHOD

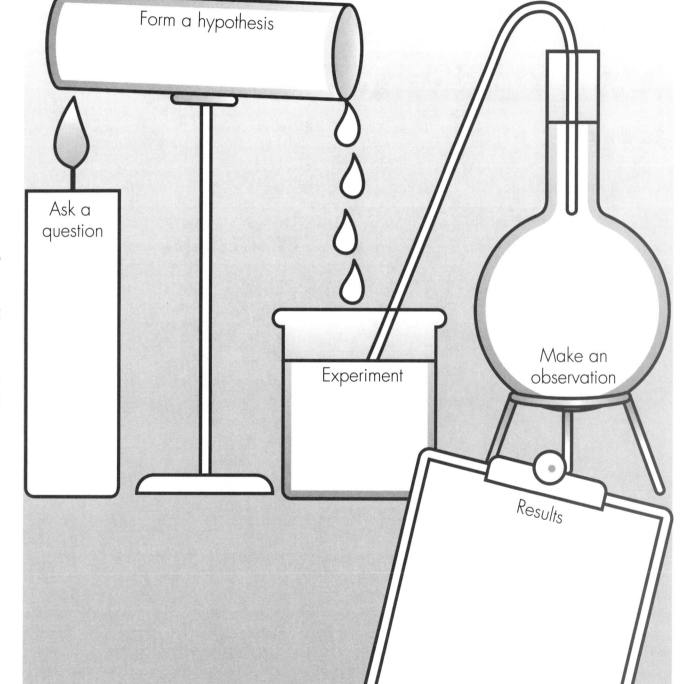

Form a hypothesis

Ask a question

Experiment

Make an observation

Results

98 Focus on a Cycle/Process

▶ Grades: K–5
▶ Level of Difficulty: Medium

Overview

This graphic organizer prompts students to identify important and critical information in a scientific cycle or sequence.

Tips for Classroom Implementation

Use the graphic organizer to model a scientific cycle like the metamorphosis of a butterfly or the life cycle of a frog. Make sure that the students include visuals and pictures to support their depictions in the graphic organizer.

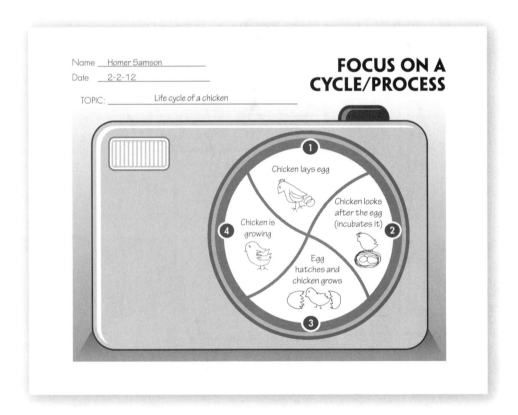

FOCUS ON A CYCLE/PROCESS

Name _____

Date _____

TOPIC: _____

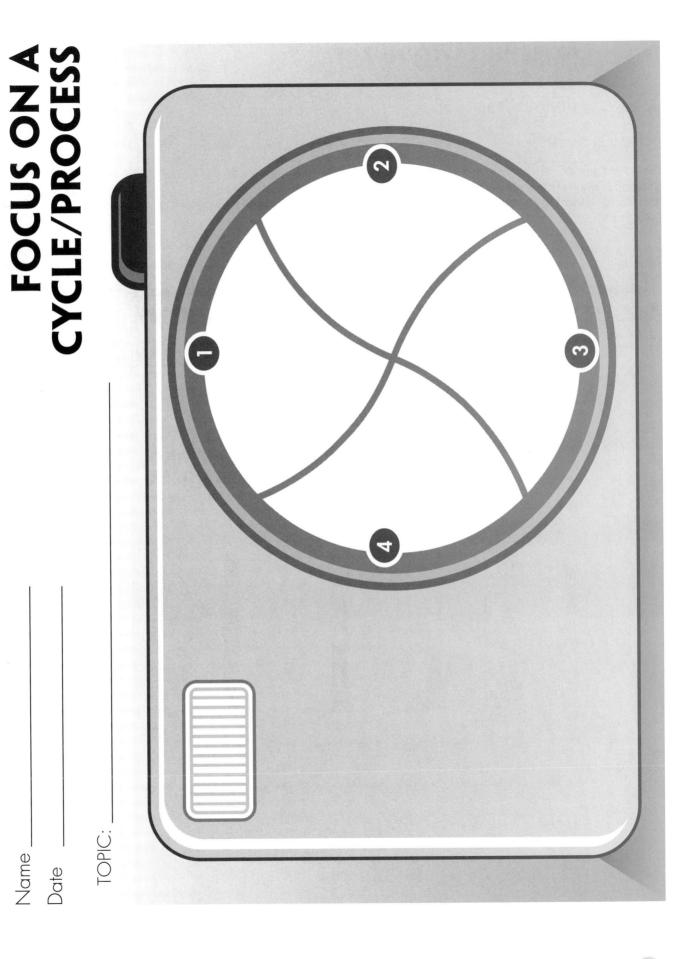

99 Graphing Organizer

► Grades: 3–5
► Level of Difficulty: Easy

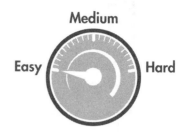

Overview

Graphing allows students to visualize information as they collect and organize data. This Graphing Organizer supports students in visually depicting information that is collected and displaying it in bar graphs, line graphs, or coordinate graphs.

Tips for Classroom Implementation

Have the students gather data about familiar items, like types of shoes, books they've read, or friends' and family members' hair color. In a large group discussion, model how to display the information on the graphic organizer. Be sure to write a title for the graph.

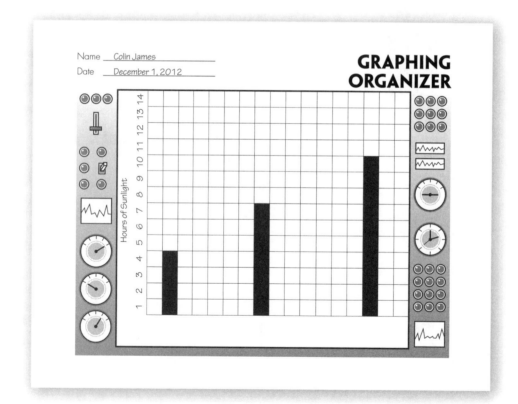

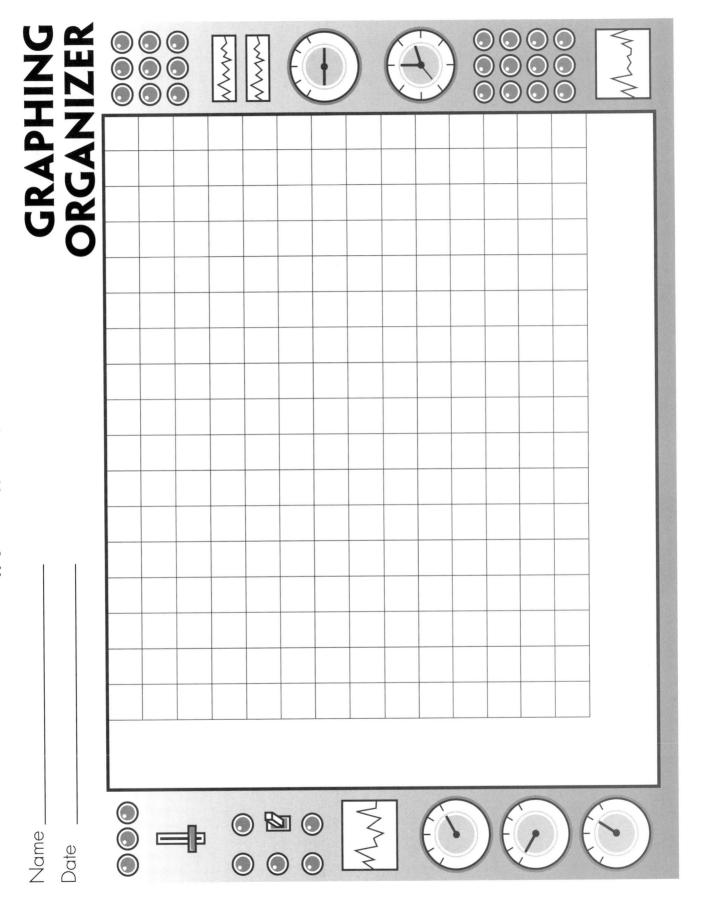

GRAPHING ORGANIZER

Name _____

Date _____

100 Quantities

▶ Grades: K–5
▶ Level of Difficulty: Easy-Medium

Overview

This graphic organizer helps students learn to identify and use equivalent numbers, expressions, and measurements. As students explore these concepts, creating visual models will support their understanding of these important mathematical concepts.

Tips for Classroom Implementation

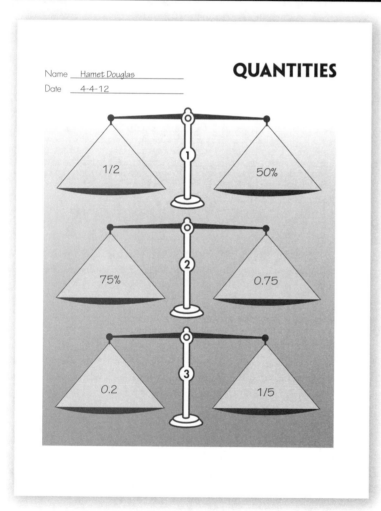

Model for the students: use manipulatives to demonstrate how to create equal quantities. You can also draw equal quantities for the students and discuss the equivalency.

Name _____

Date _____

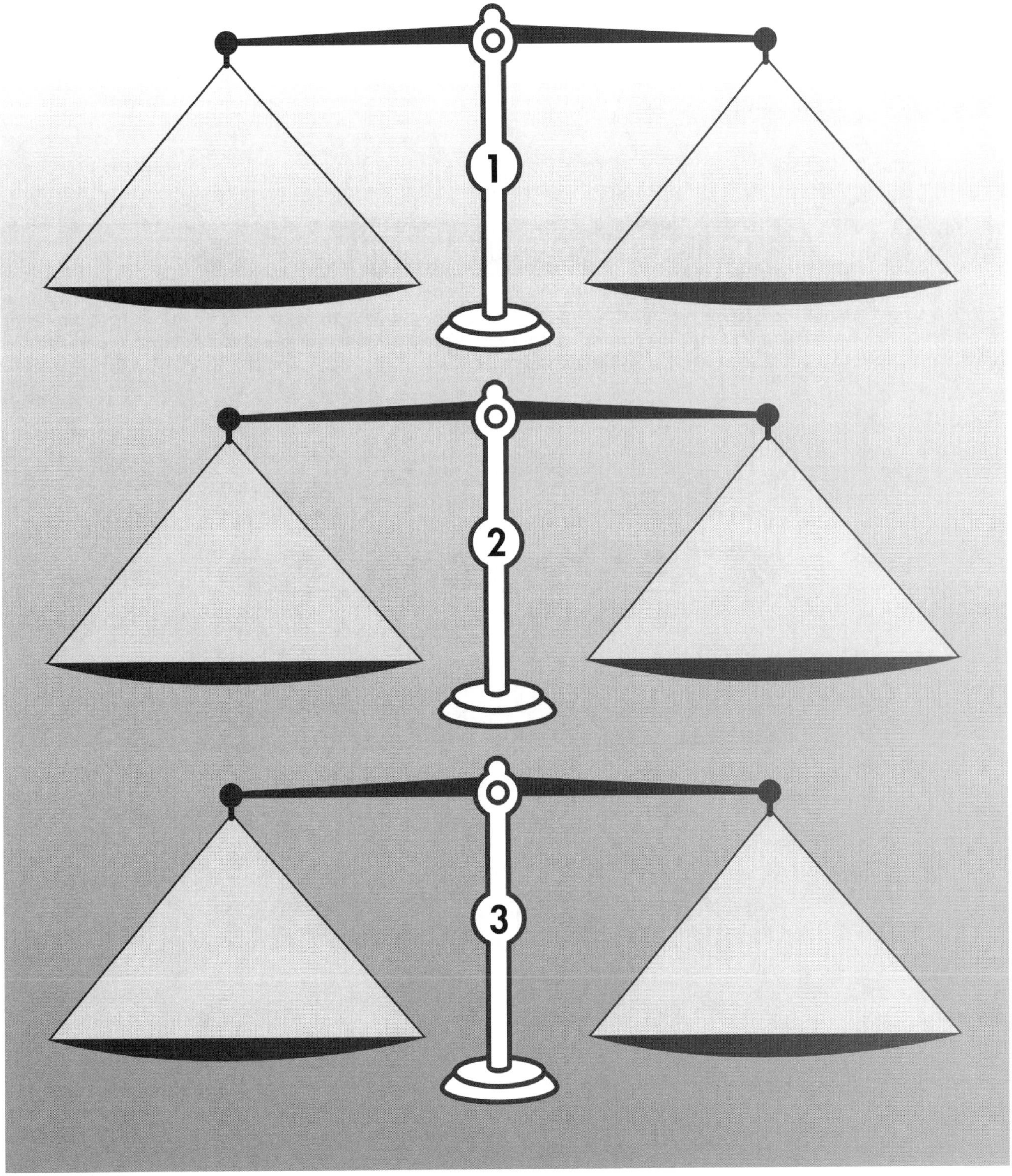

1

2

3

101 Number Placement

▶ Grades: K–5
▶ Level of Difficulty: Easy

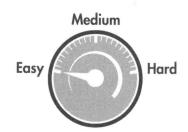

Overview

A critical mathematical concept, place value is strongly related to developing students' computation skills. This graphic organizer supports students to visualize place-value models.

Tips for Classroom Implementation

Create a larger copy of the graphic organizer for the students. This can be accomplished with an overhead projector or an interactive whiteboard, or simply by recreating it on a chalkboard. Model for the students how to complete the graphic organizer to indicate place value with various examples.

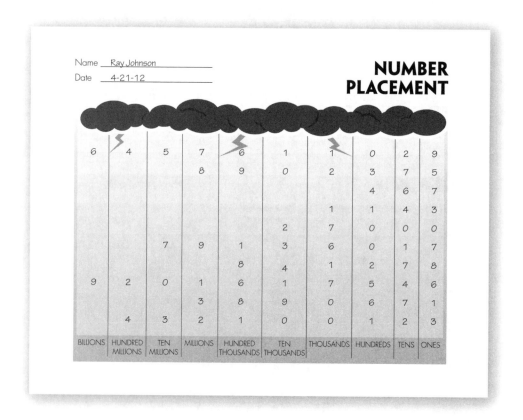

Name: Ray Johnson
Date: 4-21-12

NUMBER PLACEMENT

BILLIONS	HUNDRED MILLIONS	TEN MILLIONS	MILLIONS	HUNDRED THOUSANDS	TEN THOUSANDS	THOUSANDS	HUNDREDS	TENS	ONES
6	4	5	7	6	1	1	0	2	9
			8	9	0	2	3	7	5
							4	6	7
					1	1	1	4	3
				2	7	0	0	0	0
	7	9	1	3	6	0	1	7
			8	4	1	2	7	8
9	2	0	1	6	1	7	5	4	6
		3	8	9	0	6	7	1
	4	3	2	1	0	0	1	2	3

NUMBER PLACEMENT

Name _____

Date _____

BILLIONS	HUNDRED MILLIONS	TEN MILLIONS	MILLIONS	HUNDRED THOUSANDS	TEN THOUSANDS	THOUSANDS	HUNDREDS	TENS	ONES

102 Word Problem Solver

▶ Grades: 3–5
▶ Level of Difficulty: Medium-Hard

Overview

Word problems are some of the most challenging teaching and learning activities. This Word Problem Solver helps students to identify and organize the information from a word problem so that it can be more easily solved.

Tips for Classroom Implementation

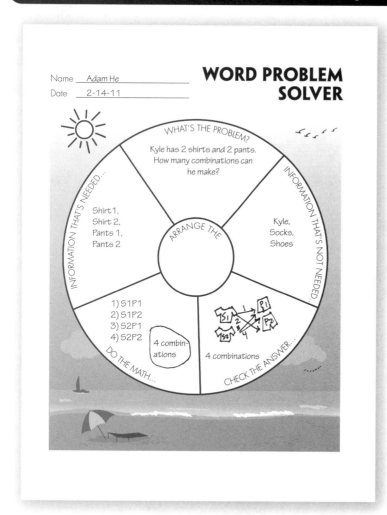

Model for the students how to use this graphic organizer. When I introduce or discuss word problems, I think it is especially helpful for students to highlight key information. From the highlighted key information, have the students record the corresponding information in the prompts that are included in the graphic organizer. All students will benefit from sketching and visually representing the key information, but it is especially critical for younger students.

Name _____

Date _____

WORD PROBLEM SOLVER

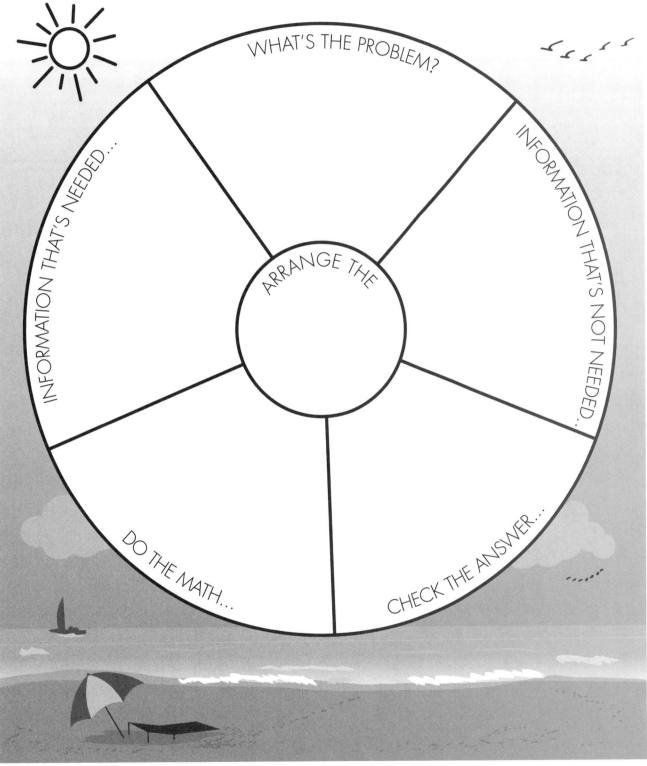

WHAT'S THE PROBLEM?

INFORMATION THAT'S NEEDED...

INFORMATION THAT'S NOT NEEDED...

ARRANGE THE

DO THE MATH...

CHECK THE ANSWER...

103 Equation Detective

▶ Grades: 3–5
▶ Level of Difficulty: Hard

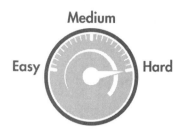

Overview

The Equation Detective is a graphic organizer that helps students to record and discover equations that can equal one number. The organizer includes the following operations: addition, subtraction, multiplication, and division.

Tips for Classroom Implementation

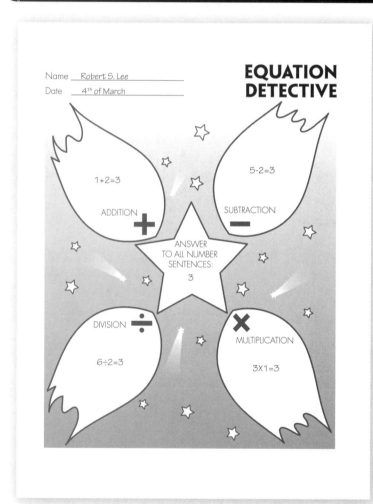

In the space provided, decide on a number. The students will use each of the operations—addition, subtraction, multiplication, and division—to create equations that equal the decided number. Younger students can represent the quantities through pictures and visual representations.

Name _____

Date _____

EQUATION DETECTIVE

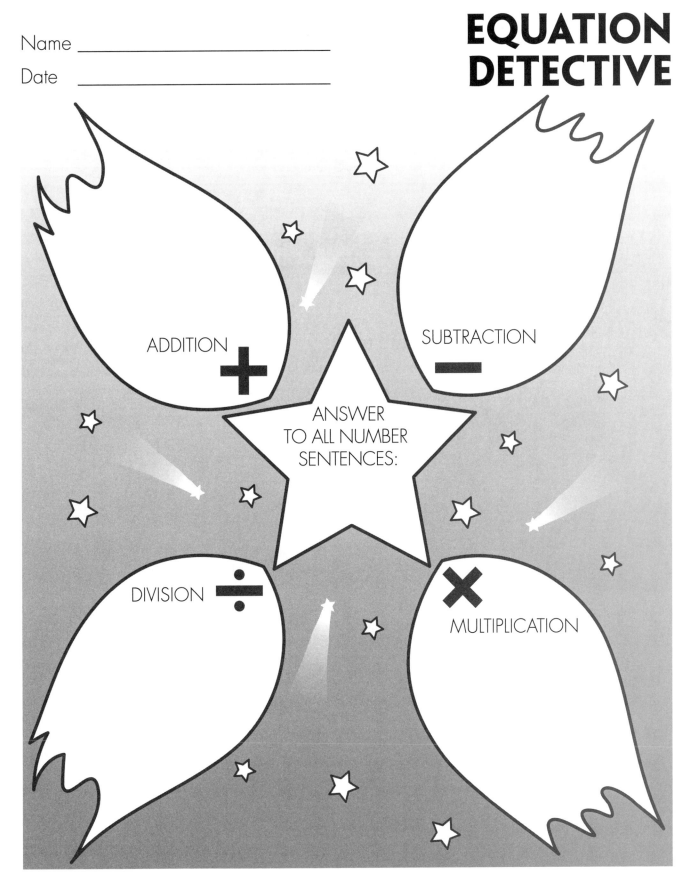

ADDITION **+**

SUBTRACTION **—**

ANSWER
TO ALL NUMBER
SENTENCES:

DIVISION **÷**

✖ MULTIPLICATION

104 Math Factors

▶ Grades: K–5
▶ Level of Difficulty: Medium-Hard

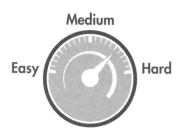

Overview

The Math Factors graphic organizer supports students' understanding in determining the different factors that can make up a number.

Tips for Classroom Implementation

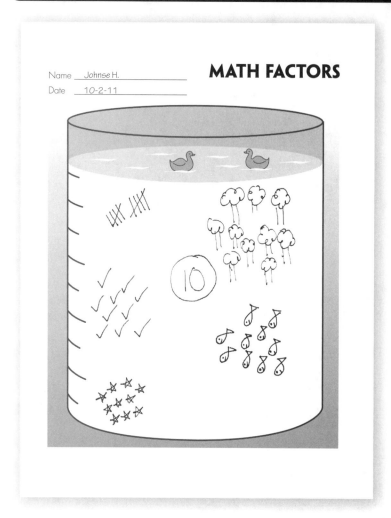

In a large group discussion, review the concept of factors with the students. Have the students select a number that will be recorded in the center of the graphic organizer. Prompt the students to consider all of the possible factors that can equal the number in the middle of the graphic organizer. Younger students can use pictures or tallies to represent the different factors.

Name _____

Date _____

MATH FACTORS

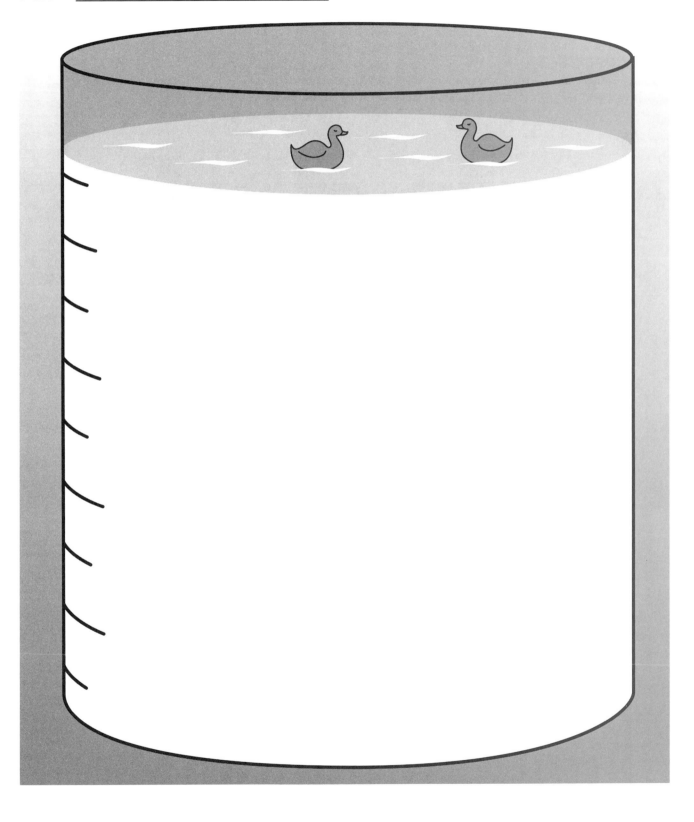

105 Pie Organizer

▶ Grades: K–5
▶ Level of Difficulty: Medium-Hard

Overview

Similar to the Graphing Organizer, the Pie Organizer helps students to organize and display data visually. The pie chart supports students in identifying and representing the relationships between individual parts and a whole, as in fractions.

Tips for Classroom Implementation

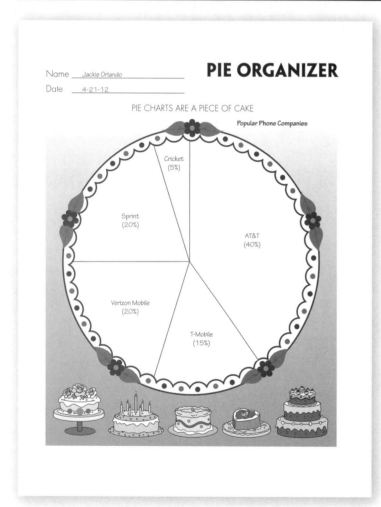

Model for the students how to divide the Pie Organizer into different parts. Explain to the students that the entire pie is equal to 100 percent and that each section is a percentage of that total. Use some data that will likely be of interest to the students, like identifying their favorite ice cream flavors or their favorite colors.